Understanding Psychological Health

This book draws on Rational Emotive Behaviour Therapy (REBT) – which focuses on resolving emotional and behavioural problems and disturbances and enables people to lead happier and more fulfilling lives – to provide an understanding of psychological health. Each chapter looks at an important aspect of psychological health and then discusses it in relation to the REBT approach.

Divided into two parts the book looks first at how people can remain psychologically healthy in the face of adversity and then goes on to discuss how these healthy philosophies underpin certain key areas of psychological health. As such, topics of discussion include:

- flexibility
- acceptance
- self-motivation
- resilience.

Understanding Psychological Health will be of great interest to all therapists in both practice and training.

Windy Dryden is Professor of Psychotherapeutic Studies at Goldsmiths, University of London.

Understanding Psychological Health

The REBT Perspective

Windy Dryden

Routledge
Taylor & Francis Group

LONDON AND NEW YORK

First published 2011 by Routledge
27 Church Road, Hove, East Sussex BN3 2FA

Simultaneously published in the USA and Canada
by Routledge
270 Madison Avenue, New York, NY 10016

Routledge is an imprint of the Taylor & Francis Group, an Informa business

© 2011 Windy Dryden

Typeset in Times by Garfield Morgan, Swansea, West Glamorgan
Printed and bound in Great Britain by TJ International Ltd, Padstow,
Cornwall
Cover design by Andrew Ward

This publication has been produced with paper manufactured to strict
environmental standards and with pulp derived from sustainable forests.

British Library Cataloguing in Publication Data
A catalogue record for this book is available from the British Library

Library of Congress Cataloging-in-Publication Data
Dryden, Windy.
    Understanding psychological health : the REBT perspective / Windy
Dryden.
        p. ; cm.
    ISBN 978-0-415-56634-6 (hbk.) – ISBN 978-0-415-56635-3 (pbk.) 1.
Rational emotive behavior therapy. 2. Mental health. I. Title.
    [DNLM: 1. Psychotherapy, Rational-Emotive. 2. Adaptation,
Psychological. 3. Mental Health. WM 420.5.P8 D799ua 2010]
    RC489.R3D825 2010
    616.89'14–dc22

                                                            2010017316

ISBN: 978-0-415-56634-6 (hbk)
ISBN: 978-0-415-56635-3 (pbk)

Contents

Preface   vii

1 Psychological health: from disturbance to
   dissatisfaction and development   1

PART 1
The basics of psychological health: being healthy
in the face of adversity   5

2 Flexibility   7

3 Non-awfulising   30

4 Discomfort tolerance   44

5 Acceptance   61

PART 2
Psychological health: beyond the basics   87

6 Self-motivation   89

7 Self-discipline   107

8 Resilience   120

9 Tolerance of uncertainty   142

10 Self-control 158

References 173
Index 174

Preface

This book follows up and complements my previous book for Routledge entitled *Understanding Emotional Problems: The REBT Perspective* (Dryden, 2009a). In each chapter, I will consider an important ingredient of psychological health and will discuss the salient issues from an REBT perspective. This is the first book on understanding psychological health written from an REBT perspective and as such it is unique. The book is divided into two parts.

The first part of the book will be devoted to how people can remain psychologically healthy in the face of adversity. I will outline REBT's well-known position on rational beliefs, but couch this in the form of healthy rational philosophies that underpin constructive action and subsequent realistic thinking.

In the second part of the book, I will discuss how these healthy rational philosophies underpin certain key areas of psychological health. Throughout this part of the book I will stress a realistic, rather than an ideal view of psychological health and I will thus end each chapter with what I call a realistic rational credo for each area. Since some readers may only consult certain rather than all chapters, I end each chapter with the same brief discussion of the credo in question.

Windy Dryden
London and Eastbourne
July, 2010

Chapter 1

Psychological health: from disturbance to dissatisfaction and development

Levels of problems

One of the defining characteristics of human beings is that we experience problems, and these problems can be viewed from an REBT perspective as existing at different levels. Indeed, one of the distinctive features of REBT is its position on these different problems and the order in which they should be addressed (Dryden, 2009b).

Thus, people have *emotional problems* where we disturb ourselves about the presence of adversities in our lives. When we deal effectively with our disturbance, we still have *dissatisfaction problems* about the existence of these adversities. If we are successful at changing these adversities, if they can be changed, or at adjusting constructively to the existence of these adversities if they cannot be changed, then we may experience *development problems*. Here, while we are not facing life's adversities we have a sense that we are not fulfilling our potential in life.

As I said earlier, one distinctive feature of REBT is that it outlines a logical order for dealing with these problems.

Tackling disturbance before dissatisfaction

REBT argues that unless there are good reasons to the contrary, people should address their emotional problems before their dissatisfaction problems. The reasoning here is as follows: if we try to deal with our dissatisfaction before we deal with our emotional disturbance, then our disturbed feelings will get in the way of our efforts to change directly the adversities about which we are dissatisfied.

For example, let's take the example of Paul who is dissatisfied about his wife's spending habits. However, he is also unhealthily angry about her behaviour and every time he talks to her about it he makes himself angry, raises his voice and makes pejorative remarks about her and her spending behaviour. Now what is the likely impact of Paul's expression of unhealthy anger on his wife? Does it encourage her to stand back and look objectively at her own behaviour? Of course, it doesn't. Paul's angry behaviour is more likely to lead his wife to become unhealthily angry herself and/or to become defensive. In Paul's case, his anger had, in fact, both effects on his wife. Now, let's suppose that Paul *first* addressed his unhealthy anger and then discussed his dissatisfaction with his wife. His annoyance at her behaviour, but his acceptance of her as a person, would help him to view her behaviour perhaps as a sign of emotional disturbance and his compassion for her would have very different effects on her. She would probably be less defensive, and because Paul would not be unhealthily angry, his wife would also be less likely to be unhealthily angry herself. With anger out of the picture, the stage would be set for Paul to address the reasons for his dissatisfaction more effectively.

Tackling disturbance before development

In the late 1960s and early 1970s, I used to go to a number of encounter groups. This was the era of personal growth and development. However, there were a number of casualties of these groups and when these occurred it was because attendees were preoccupied with issues of emotional disturbance and they were being pushed too hard to go into areas of development that warranted greater resilience.

In general, then, it is very difficult for us to develop ourselves when we are emotionally disturbed. To focus on areas of development when we are emotionally disturbed is akin to us climbing a very steep hill with very heavy weights attached to our ankles. First, we need to remove our ankle weights (i.e. address our emotional disturbance) before thinking about the best way of climbing the hill.

For example, Fiona wanted to become a really good public speaker and, to further her goal, she enrolled on a 'Become a Master Speaker' training course. However, Fiona was very anxious about public speaking because she was scared of becoming tongue-tied and losing her way. This anxiety quickly surfaced on the training course and the tutors advised her to seek therapeutic help first since, as they told her, she would be unlikely to develop her public speaking skills until she had dealt effectively with her anxiety. Taking their advice, Fiona sought help from an REBT therapist and developed a set of healthy beliefs about the possibility of becoming tongue-tied and losing her way while talking in public. Armed with a new set of healthy beliefs, Fiona re-enrolled on the 'Become a Master Speaker' training course and developed her skills in this area.

Tackling dissatisfaction before development

Abraham Maslow (1968) is perhaps best known for his work on self-actualisation. The relevance of this concept for our present discussion is this. It is very difficult for us as humans to focus on our higher-order 'needs' while we are preoccupied with issues with respect to our lower-order 'needs'. Thus, if a person is faced with an adversity which he (in this case) cannot compartmentalise in his mind and that person also wants to explore his writing ambitions, then he needs first to address this adversity, even if he holds a set of healthy beliefs about it, unless the presence of the adversity will help him write a better book!

The scope of this book

This book is divided into two major parts. In the first part of the book, I will outline how we can become psychologically healthy in the face of life's adversities. This is where you need to start if you are, in fact, disturbing yourself about such adversities. In this part of the book, I will be dealing with the heart of REBT's position on psychological health. In brief, we are psychologically healthy about life's adversities to the extent that we:

- hold flexible (as opposed to rigid) beliefs about life's adversities
- hold non-awfulising (as opposed to awfulising) beliefs about the adversities
- believe that we are able to tolerate (as opposed to not tolerate) the discomfort of facing these adversities

- adopt an accepting (as opposed to a depreciating) attitude towards ourselves, other people and life conditions as these relate to the adversities.

In the second part of the book, I will show how we can employ the above healthy beliefs in the following areas of personal development: self-motivation, self-discipline, resilience, tolerance of uncertainty and self-control.

Taken together, then, the two parts of this book present REBT's position on psychological health which takes this therapeutic approach out of the consulting room into everyday life where it can potentially make its most profound contribution to health and well-being.

Part 1

The basics of psychological health: being healthy in the face of adversity

Chapter 2

Flexibility

Introduction

In this chapter and the three that follow, I will discuss the four cornerstones of a psychologically healthy response to the presence of life's adversities. The view that I will be propounding in these four chapters and that permeates the rest of the book is based on the pioneering work of Dr Albert Ellis (1913–2007), the founder of a therapeutic approach known as Rational Emotive Behaviour Therapy (REBT).

Ellis's work on the conceptualisation of emotional problems (which I discuss fully in the companion to this volume – Dryden, 2009a) extended Epictetus's maxim that 'People are disturbed not by things but by their views of things'. Ellis argued that such 'views' are best understood as irrational beliefs that are illogical, empirically false and lead largely to poor results for the person holding them.

Ellis argues that there are four such irrational beliefs. In brief, we disturb ourselves about life's adversities to the extent that we:

- hold rigid (as opposed to flexible) beliefs about life's adversities
- hold awfulising (as opposed to non-awfulising) beliefs about the adversities
- believe that we are unable to tolerate (as opposed to tolerate) the discomfort of facing these adversities
- adopt a depreciating (as opposed to an accepting) attitude towards ourselves, other people and life conditions as these relate to the adversities.

As I showed in Chapter 1, we deal with the same adversities in a healthy way to the extent that we:

- hold flexible (as opposed to rigid) beliefs about life's adversities
- hold non-awfulising (as opposed to awfulising) beliefs about the adversities
- believe that we are able to tolerate (as opposed to not tolerate) the discomfort of facing these adversities
- adopt an accepting (as opposed to a depreciating) attitude towards ourselves, other people and life conditions as these relate to the adversities.

Ellis (1994) argued that of the four healthy beliefs mentioned above flexible beliefs are at the very core of a healthy response to life's adversities and that the other three are derived from this flexible core. In this chapter, I will concentrate on the concept of flexibility, and I will discuss the other derived healthy beliefs in the following three chapters.

The two basic components of flexible beliefs

In this section, I will discuss the two basic components of flexible beliefs: a preferential component and a non-rigid component.

The preferential component of flexible beliefs

Aside from fallibility, which I will discuss in Chapter 5, perhaps the defining characteristic of human beings is that we have likes and dislikes.

Positive and negative preferences

We are oriented towards certain things because we prefer them to happen. I call such preferences 'positive preferences' because they articulate our desires for the presence of things to which we assign a positive value. Conversely, we are oriented away from other things because we prefer them not to happen. I call such preferences 'negative preferences' because they articulate our desires for the absence of things to which we assign a negative value.

We differ markedly in the content of our preferences

While holding positive and negative preferences is a defining aspect of being human, we differ markedly concerning the content of these preferences. Thus, some of us prefer an element of risk and seek out events precisely because they give us this desired element, while others of us prefer this element of risk to be absent and seek out events which are free from this undesired element.

Preferences vary along a strength continuum

Our preferences can vary along a continuum of strength in that we can hold a mild preference for something (e.g. 'I mildly want to beat you at tiddlywinks') or a very strong preference for something (e.g. 'I very much want to be promoted at work').

A defining feature of REBT as a therapeutic approach is that when someone is disturbed about an adversity (e.g. the person has failed to be promoted at work) the REBT therapist does not attempt to encourage the person to reduce the strength of his (in this case) positive preference for being promoted. This is because the REBT view of psychological disturbance holds that such disturbance is not a consequence of unmet preferences, no matter how strong these preferences are. Rather, REBT holds that such disturbance stems from unmet demands. I will discuss this further later in this chapter. Thus, there is nothing intrinsically disturbing in the fact that the person holds a very strong positive preference to be promoted. It follows that if the therapist attempts to help the person to reduce the strength of his preference, then the therapist will not help him to address the source of his disturbance. Rather, the therapist will be encouraging the person to lie to himself, to persuade himself that the strength of his positive preference is not as strong as it actually is.

REBT theory holds that passion is defined by very strong preferences and the goal of interventions designed to promote psychological health should not be to help people to reduce passion but to maintain passion and minimise disturbance. I will also discuss this issue further later in this chapter.

The preferential component is present in a rigid belief

So far, I have discussed the preferential component of flexible beliefs. However, this component is also present in rigid beliefs. Let's take the case of Erica. It is very important for her to get a place on a prestigious Ph.D. programme. However, she is also very anxious about the possibility that she may not gain entry into this programme. REBT theory holds that it is not the strength of Erica's preference that explains her anxiety. This preference is stated thus: 'I very much want to get onto the Ph.D. programme.' Erica becomes anxious when she transforms her preferential component into a rigid belief, thus: 'I very much want to get onto the Ph.D. programme and therefore I must do so.' While this rigid belief is usually articulated with the preference component omitted (e.g. 'I must get onto the Ph.D. programme'), as we have seen, this rigid belief is actually comprised of a preferential component and a rigid component.

As discussed later in this chapter, a flexible belief is also comprised of two components: a preferential component and a non-rigid component. This latter component actively states that the person concerned does not transform the preferential component into a rigidity. Thus, if we return to Erica's example, in being helped to develop a flexible belief she was encouraged to maintain the strength of her preference, but to negate the rigid component of her rigid belief. Her new flexible belief was thus: 'I very much want to get onto the Ph.D. programme, but I don't have to do so.' This latter component ('. . . but I don't have to do so') is the one that determines Erica's new healthy response of concern about the prospect of not getting onto the Ph.D. programme.

Table 1 makes the point that it is the rigid component that underpins Erica's feelings of anxiety, while it is the non-rigid component that underpins her feelings of concern. This table shows clearly that the preferential component is the same for both beliefs.

Table 1 Flexible and rigid beliefs, their components and their emotional consequences

Rigid belief	Preferential component	Rigid component	Emotion
'I must get onto the Ph.D. programme'	'I very much want to get onto the Ph.D. programme . . .	. . . and therefore I have to get onto it'	Anxiety

Flexible belief	Preferential component	Non-rigid component	Emotion
'I very much want to get onto the Ph.D. programme, but I don't have to do so'	'I very much want to get onto the Ph.D. programme . . .	. . . but I don't have to do so'	Concern

Active vs. passive preferences

It is useful to distinguish between active preferences and passive preferences. Active preferences are those preferences that you are prepared to take action on while passive preferences indicate the conditions that you would like to exist but which you are not prepared to take action on in order to achieve. Take the cases of Melvin and Stuart who both would like to run a marathon. Melvin's preference is active in that he finds out what he needs to do to run a marathon and acts on this knowledge, while Stuart's preference is passive in that he takes no steps to achieve it. Asked why he does not do anything to fulfil his desire, Stuart says that he wants to run a marathon and plans to do this one day. Thus, the existence of passive preferences (where the idea of planning to take action is pushed into the future) may be a sign that the person is procrastinating.

I noted earlier that preferences vary along a strength continuum. It may well be the case that active preferences are stronger than passive preferences. Thus, we may find that Melvin's preference to run a marathon is stronger than Stuart's. However, this is not always the case and it may be that Stuart's desire is stronger than Melvin's, but that Melvin is more prepared to act on his weaker preference than Stuart is on his stronger preference.

It is also worth noting that as soon as a person acts on a preference that he previously had not acted on, that person's passive preference becomes an active preference.

The non-rigid component of flexible beliefs

I made the point above that rigid and flexible beliefs both contain a preferential component. Thus, this component does not differentiate between these beliefs. It is the second component that is the important component in helping us to distinguish between these two beliefs.

Understanding the non-rigid component of a flexible belief by first understanding the rigid component of a rigid belief

One can best understand the non-rigid component of a flexible belief by first understanding the rigid component of a rigid belief.

As Table 1 shows (see p. 10), a belief becomes rigid when the person transforms her (in this case) preferential component into a rigidity. Thus, in her rigid belief, Erica begins by acknowledging: 'I very much want to get onto the Ph.D. programme . . .' Then she transforms this preferential component into a rigid belief by adding the rigid component: '. . . and therefore I have to do so'. You will note from Table 1 that a rigid belief is often expressed with the preferential component omitted ('I must get onto the Ph.D. programme'). This is why I have deconstructed the rigid belief to show how the person adds the rigid component to the preferential component to create her rigid belief. Thus:

> Preferential component + Rigid component = Rigid belief

The nature of a non-rigid component

As the name makes clear the basic nature of a non-rigid component of a flexible belief is that it is not rigid. Thus, when it is articulated, the person needs to make clear that she (in this case) is explicitly stating that rigidity is not present in the flexible belief. In Erica's case, you will see that she first states the preferential component of her flexible belief: 'I very much want to get onto the Ph.D. programme . . .' Then by adding the non-rigid component of her flexible belief ('. . . but I don't have to do so'), she very explicitly states that rigidity is not present in this belief and it is therefore flexible. Thus:

> Preferential component + Non-rigid component
> = Flexible belief

Here are other examples of non-rigid components. These are underlined in the following flexible beliefs:

- 'I want you to love me, but you don't have to do so.'
- 'I want life to be easier for me, but it does not have to be the way I want it to be.'

Preferences: full and part

In REBT theory, flexible belief alternatives to rigid beliefs are frequently referred to as preferences. However, this increases the chances that a person does not appreciate the fundamental non-rigid nature of flexible beliefs.

Thus, when training novice REBT therapists, I ask them to give me examples of healthy alternatives to rigid beliefs. Frequently their answers are examples of what I call 'part or partial preferences' rather than 'full preferences' (or what I frequently call non-dogmatic preferences for a reason I will discuss presently).

Part (or partial) preferences are essentially the preferential components of flexible beliefs, as shown in the following examples:

- 'I want you to love me.'
- 'I want life to be easier for me.'

As my analysis of flexible beliefs in this chapter shows, we are not sure if these partial preferences are flexible or not. Since partial preferences lack an explicit non-rigid component, the following possibilities exist:

1 A partial preference is flexible and the non-rigid component is present, but unstated. Here, the person truly believes the following:
- 'I want you to love me, but you don't have to do so.'
- 'I want life to be easier for me, but it does not have to be the way I want it to be.'

Please note that in the above beliefs, the unstated components are underlined.

2 A partial preference is rigid and the person transforms the partial component into a rigidity, but does this implicitly without stating that he has done so. Here the person truly believes the following:
- 'I want you to love me, and therefore you have to do so.'
- 'I want life to be easier for me, and therefore it has to be the way I want it to be.'

Again, please note that the unstated components above are underlined.

Because partial preferences are so unclear, it is important to express flexible beliefs in their full form (i.e. with both the preferential component and the non-rigid component being clearly stated). This is why flexible beliefs are sometimes referred to as full preferences because the full form of such flexible beliefs is clearly and explicitly stated.

Determining whether a belief is flexible or rigid

A well-known saying has it that it is better to judge people by their actions rather than by their words. This is true when attempting to ascertain whether a person holds a flexible belief or a rigid belief. Thus, it frequently happens that a person claims to hold a flexible belief when, in reality, he (in this case) actually holds this belief in its rigid form. There are many reasons why a person may claim to hold a belief in its flexible rather than in its rigid form. These reasons include: wishing to create a favourable impression; feeling ashamed to admit to holding a rigid belief; and not wishing to deal with the implications of admitting to a rigid belief. Such reasons should not preoccupy us here. What is more important is this. If a verbal report of the flexibility or rigidity of a belief is problematic, is there a more reliable way of determining whether the belief that a person holds is flexible or rigid? In my opinion there is. It is by examining the likely effects of these respective beliefs.

The emotional effects of flexible and rigid beliefs

The theory of Rational Emotive Behaviour Therapy states that if a person holds a flexible belief about an adversity then she (in this case) will experience emotions that are negative in tone, but that are largely constructive in their effects. In REBT theory these emotions are known as healthy negative emotions (HNEs). By contrast, if the person holds a rigid belief about the same adversity then she will experience emotions that will also be negative in tone, but largely unconstructive in their effects (see Dryden, 2009a, for a full discussion of what are called unhealthy negative emotions – UNEs – in REBT theory).

Let me provide an example. Two friends, Cynthia and Linda, were made redundant from their jobs in the same company on the same day. Their jobs were equally important to them and therefore the loss of their jobs was equivalent in meaning to both. However, while Cynthia was depressed about the loss, Linda was sad, but not depressed about it. According to REBT theory depression is an unhealthy negative emotion (UNE), while sadness is a healthy negative emotion (HNE). Furthermore, REBT theory states that depression stems from a rigid belief while sadness stems from a flexible belief. This was certainly true in the case of Cynthia and Linda. Cynthia was depressed largely because she rigidly demanded that she not be made redundant, while Linda was sad largely because she flexibly held that while she would have much preferred not being made redundant, she did not have to be exempt from this happening to her.

The behavioural effects of flexible and rigid beliefs

The theory of REBT also states that if a person holds a flexible belief about an adversity, then she will tend to act in ways that are largely healthy and help her to constructively change the adversity if it can be changed and to make a constructive adaptation to the situation if the adversity cannot be changed. By contrast, if the person holds a rigid belief about the same adversity, then she will tend to act in ways that are largely unhealthy which will impede her from changing the adversity in constructive ways. Also, holding the rigid belief tends to prevent the person from making a constructive adaptation to the situation if the adversity cannot be changed.

Applying this to the cases of Cynthia and Linda, we see the following. You will remember that Cynthia was depressed largely because she held a rigid belief about being made redundant. This led her to withdraw into herself and not make any attempts to apply for new jobs. Rather than seek and use support from her family and friends, she claimed things were hopeless and accused people of not being sympathetic whenever they made helpful suggestions. By contrast, Linda was sad, but not depressed about being made redundant. This led her to acknowledge and work through her loss, to stay connected with others, to apply for new jobs, and to seek and use support from friends and family members. Needless to say, Linda found a new job quite quickly, whereas Cynthia remained unemployed for much longer.

The cognitive effects of flexible and rigid beliefs

The theory of REBT further states that if a person holds a flexible belief about an adversity, then she will tend to think in ways that are balanced and incorporate positive, negative and neutral elements of the situation, whereas when the person holds a rigid belief about that adversity she will tend to think in ways that are highly distorted and heavily skewed to the negative.

For example, as a result of holding a rigid belief about being made redundant, Cynthia had the following thoughts: 'I will never get another job so it's not worth trying' and 'I will end up on the scrapheap of life'. These subsequent thoughts are known as inferences and, as can be seen, they are very skewed to the negative. By contrast, as a result of holding a flexible belief about being made redundant, Linda had the following thoughts: 'Getting a job may be difficult, but if I keep trying, I will probably get one' and 'Even if I don't get a job, I can still find meaning and pleasure in life'. These thoughts are also inferences but, as you can see, they are realistic and balanced rather than highly distorted and heavily skewed to the negative.

I have summarized the above general points in Table 2 and these refer to the experiences of Cynthia and Linda in Table 3.

Table 2 The effects of holding rigid and flexible beliefs

Rigid beliefs	Flexible beliefs
• Unhealthy negative emotions	• Healthy negative emotions
• Unconstructive behaviour	• Constructive behaviour
• Highly distorted, skewed negative thinking	• Realistic and balanced thinking

Why flexible beliefs are rational or healthy

In REBT, beliefs are rational or healthy if they meet three criteria:

- They are true.
- They are logical.
- They have healthy consequences.

By these criteria, flexible beliefs are rational or healthy. Let me elaborate.

Table 3 The effects of holding rigid and flexible beliefs: the
experiences of Cynthia and Linda

Cynthia's rigid belief	Linda's flexible belief
'I must not be made redundant'	'I would prefer not to be made redundant, but I do not have to be exempt from this happening to me'
Unhealthy negative emotion	**Healthy negative emotion**
• Anxiety	• Concern
Unconstructive behaviour	**Constructive behaviour**
• Withdrawal into self	• Staying connected to others
• No attempts to apply for new jobs	• Applying for new jobs
• Not seeking and using support from family and friends, and accusing them of not being sympathetic	• Seeking and using support from family and friends
Highly distorted, skewed negative thinking	**Realistic and balanced thinking**
• 'I will never get another job so it's not worth trying'	• 'Getting a job may be difficult, but if I keep trying, I will probably get one'
• 'I will end up on the scrap heap of life'	• 'Even if I don't get a job, I can still find meaning and pleasure in life'

Flexible beliefs are true

As I have already discussed, when you hold a flexible belief (e.g. 'I want to do well at my job, but I don't have to do so') you both assert what you want and acknowledge that you don't have to have your desire met. Your preference is true in the sense that you can give reasons for your desire. Thus, in our example, you can explain why you want to do well at your job (e.g. it will help you gain advancement and it will help improve your salary). Your acknowledgement that you don't have to have your desire met is also true since if it were true that you had to do well at your job then it would follow that you would have to do so. It would not be possible for you not to do well at your job. Since such a possibility always exists then the negation of your demand is true. Since both components of your flexible belief are true it therefore follows that the belief itself is true.

Flexible beliefs are logical

As we have seen, flexible beliefs are based on a preferential component. In our example, the flexible belief contains the statement 'I want to do well at my job', which is the preferential component, and the statement 'but I don't have to do so', which negates the demand (and is the non-rigid component).

Now, if we take the two components of a flexible belief – the preferential component and the non-rigid component – you will see that the latter does follow logically from the former.

The preferential component is non-rigid and the non-rigid component is, by definition, also non-rigid. It is perfectly logical for two non-rigid components to be linked together. Thus, the statement 'I want to do well at my job' does lead logically to the statement 'but I don't have to do so'. So a flexible belief is logical because it links together two non-rigid statements.

Thus:

Flexible belief = Preferential component (non-rigid) +
Non-rigid component (non-rigid)

e.g. 'I want to do well at my job, but I don't have to do so' (flexible belief) = 'I want to do well at my job . . .' (non-rigid preferential component) + '. . . but I don't have to do so' (non-rigid component which negates the demand).

The flexible belief is logical because its non-rigid component that negates the demand follows logically from its non-rigid preferential component:

Non-rigid $\longrightarrow$ [logical] $\longrightarrow$ Non-rigid

e.g. 'I want to do well at my job . . .' (non-rigid) $\longrightarrow$ [logical] $\longrightarrow$ '. . . but I don't have to do so' (non-rigid).

Thus, flexible beliefs are logical.

Flexible beliefs are helpful

First, flexible beliefs tend to lead to one or more of the following healthy negative emotions when you encounter adversities at 'A': concern, sadness, remorse, disappointment, sorrow, healthy anger, healthy jealousy and healthy envy. Second, flexible beliefs tend to lead to constructive behaviour in the face of adversities such as: facing up to and dealing with difficult situations, sensible working hours, healthy exercise patterns and healthy eating and drinking patterns. Third, flexible beliefs tend to lead to subsequent realistic thinking such as making realistic estimates of adversities happening, viewing positive events as equally as likely to occur as negative events, seeing negative events in perspective and in a sensible context and making an objective appraisal of your coping resources.

Why is flexibility a central feature of psychological health?

As we have just seen, when you hold a flexible belief when facing an adversity, you will experience a number of emotional, behavioural and cognitive effects that will increase your chances of changing the adversity if it can be changed or of adjusting constructively to it if it cannot be changed. However, there are other positive aspects of flexibility that I think make it a central feature of psychological health and I will discuss these aspects in this section.

Flexibility helps you to 'roll with the punches' when hit by an adversity

In the above section, I discussed the different consequences of holding flexible and rigid beliefs. As you will have seen from that discussion, the consequences of holding flexible beliefs are healthier than those that stem from holding rigid beliefs, and I illustrated this in my discussion of the experiences of Cynthia and Linda, two women who were made redundant from the same job on the same day, but who held different beliefs about being made redundant. Table 3 outlined their different beliefs and the different consequences that flowed from these different beliefs.

One point is clear from this material. When a person holds a flexible belief, she (in this case) is more able to 'roll with the punches' of life than if she holds a rigid belief. In boxing, a fighter who has a flexible upper body is far more able to 'roll with the punches' than a fighter with a rigid upper frame. Being able to 'roll with the punches' in boxing means that you are able to avoid being hit when this is possible and when it is not possible then you are able to minimise the effects of being hit by going with the direction of the punches rather than being static or indeed going towards the punches. A boxer with a rigid upper body, on the other hand, is far less able to 'roll with the punches' because his rigid frame restricts his movement, meaning that he is less able to avoid being hit and more likely to absorb the full force of the punches when he is hit.

If you consider the case of Cynthia above, her rigid belief led her to absorb the full force of the adversity and restricted her cognitive and behavioural movement in responding to it. Her response was akin to being knocked out by being made redundant, although in reality the knock-out blow came more from the rigid belief she held about the adversity than from the adversity itself. This is apparent when one looks at the case of Linda who experienced the same redundancy and who attributed the same level of importance to the loss as Cynthia did. Linda's flexible belief enabled her to 'ride with the punch' of being made redundant and while she was knocked down by the experience she was not knocked out by it. Climbing off the canvas, her flexible belief enabled Linda to think about how to respond to life after being hit with the adversity. By contrast, Cynthia's rigid belief led her to disengage from the process of thinking how best to get on with her life.

I will consider the role of flexible beliefs in helping you to deal constructively with adversity in the chapter on resilience (see Chapter 8).

Flexibility helps you to adjust to change

As any organisational consultant will tell you, the people in an organisation who have the toughest time dealing with change are those who hold a rigid set of ideas about how they think things in the organisation should and must be. Holding such a rigid set of beliefs motivates such people to resist change and sometimes to sabotage it. Believing that they know how things must be in the organisation leads these people to hold black-and-white views of an 'I am right, you are wrong' nature (see de Bono, 1991, for an extended discussion of this type of black-and-white thinking). Once a person holds this type of rigid belief and the black-and-white thinking that follows from it, then she (in this case) is very likely to adopt a trenchant position which is unhealthy for her, but to which she clings almost as if her life depended on it.

Many years ago, a woman was referred to me for counselling who was off work for reasons of stress. At assessment it transpired that this woman, who was a secretary in local government, had been spending very long periods at work correcting drafts on her typewriter after staff in her office were issued with computers. With the advent of computers, all the secretarial workloads had increased since the bosses argued reasonably that word-processing packages made excessive re-typing a thing of the past. While most of the secretaries grumbled about using the new technology, all did so except my client, who steadfastly refused both to use a computer and to attend the appropriate training courses that were on offer. She maintained that typing reports had worked well for her in the past and that, in her view, reports had to be typed on a typewriter rather than on a computer. People who thought differently, she claimed, were 'just plain wrong'. Holding this rigid belief led her to adopt the only behavioural response allowed by her belief: to type and re-type drafts until they were perfect. For a while, her employers were tolerant of her stance, thinking that it would be temporary and that she would soon adjust, as all of her colleagues had done. But this did not happen, and as well as grappling with the overwork caused by her rigid stance this woman was now told that she had to use a computer or face being sacked. She could not be made redundant because her post was crucial and could not be lost.

It soon transpired that this woman only came to see me to satisfy her GP who had referred her to me and that she did not think that she had a problem. Indeed, she thought that her employers had the problem because they were doing the wrong thing and that they would come to regret it. It is not the role of the counsellor to force the 'client' to see the error of her ways. Indeed, this woman never became a client of mine in the sense that she gave informed consent to engage in a process of change designed to help her address self-defined problems.

I heard later that this woman was indeed sacked from her job since she refused to do other work generously offered to her by her employer. 'I have been a secretary all my working life and I will remain a secretary until my dying day!', she made quite clear in our one and only interview. Her words were indeed prophetic as she committed suicide not long after and left a note blaming her death on her employer.

For this woman to adjust to change, she would have had to develop a flexible belief. She would have had to hold the view that while she preferred to use a typewriter to type and re-type drafts for her employer, this practice was not set in stone and did not have to be followed at all costs. This would have led her to decide to get retrained to use computers and to use one because it was in her best interests to do so, even though she didn't like it at first. Indeed, this flexible view would have led her to develop and maintain an open mind (sadly lacking when she held her rigid belief) and thus be open to the possibility that she might get on with using a computer and even prefer it over a typewriter one day.

Flexibility helps you to initiate constructive change

In the above section, I argued that holding a flexible belief helps a person to adjust to change. It also helps a person to initiate change when it is for the better. I will explain this by first considering two rigid beliefs that block people from initiating constructive change. The first is expressed in a form similar to this: 'I must have the comfort of what is familiar to me even if it does not work too well.' This results in the person 'making do' with the status quo when it would be in the person's best interests to initiate change. The healthy flexible alternative to this belief is as follows: 'I prefer the comfort of what is familiar to me, but I don't have to have such comfort.' This results in the person (a) initiating change when it is in his best interests to do so, even though it means that he will experience discomfort in doing so, and (b) remaining with the status quo when it is clear that it is better than the newer alternative.

The other rigid belief is expressed in a form similar to this: 'I must have the excitement of the novel.' This belief leads the person to infer that the novel is invariably better than the status quo, even when it is not, and to initiate changes that are not warranted. The healthy, flexible alternative belief is as follows: 'I like the excitement of the novel, but I do not need to have it.' This results in the person making an objective appraisal of both the value of the new and the value of the status quo and initiating change if it provides better value.

Flexibility helps you to embrace complexity

We live in a complex world and thus we need a set of beliefs that enable us to deal with such complexity. Rigid beliefs do not help us to do this since they reduce the world into overly simple black-and-white categories. Let's take a commonly held rigid belief that underpins guilt, for example, and apply it to the case of Richard.

Richard held the following rigid guilt-inducing belief: 'When I am involved, I must not do anything that could possibly contribute to any harm coming to any of my friends or family and if I do then I am totally to blame for that harm.' One day, Richard received invitations from two friends to attend different parties in different parts of the country on the same day. It was not practicable for him to attend both parties so he had to let one of his friends down. Richard was racked with guilt because whichever way he turned he would consider himself to be a bad person for causing upset to one of his friends.

Richard's rigid belief led him to see the situation in the following simple terms:

- If I hurt a friend, I am a bad person.
- I am bound to hurt at least one friend.
- I am totally responsible for that hurt.
- I cannot escape being a bad person.

Now let's consider the flexible alternative to that rigid belief: 'When I am involved, I would prefer not to do anything that could possibly contribute to any harm coming to any of my friends or family, but sadly I am not immune from doing so and there is no universal law that states that I must have that immunity. If I do contribute to that harm, I will take responsibility for my actions, but I am rarely totally to blame for that harm.'

As we will see, this flexible belief does allow for the person holding it to view the world in more complex terms. So, let's revisit the case of Richard and consider how holding the flexible belief would have led him to view the situation where he could not avoid letting down one of his friends:

- If I hurt a friend, I am not a bad person. Rather I am a fallible human being who did a bad thing.
- I am not necessarily bound to hurt at least one friend. Once I have made my decision, I will explain that to the friend whose party I have decided not to attend and hopefully he will understand my decision.
- However, if that friend does feel hurt, I am not totally responsible for that hurt. I am responsible for my decision and the

way I have chosen to inform him of that decision, but he is also responsible for how he responds to my explanation. This is the case no matter which friend I choose to let down.

- I can escape being a bad person since my identity is not defined by the feelings of the friend I have chosen to let down.

Flexibility promotes creativity

The final healthy consequence of holding flexible beliefs that I wish to discuss is creativity. While creativity depends on being knowledgeable and skilled in the area in question, it can readily be promoted or impeded by the belief that a person holds. Holding a rigid belief leads to a closed mind which is the antithesis of creativity. Thus, if you hold one or more of the following beliefs, then it will be difficult for you to think and/or act creatively:

- 'The creative process must be effortless.'

(If you hold this belief then you will, in all probability, not even initiate the creative process, since it is often one that does involve discomfort.)

- 'My ideas must make sense to me and/or others.'

(People who are creative often report that for every one sensible creative idea that they have, they will have many more which will not make sense. Such individuals accept this and continue with their pursuit of sensible creative ideas even though previous ideas do not make sense to themselves or to others. Indeed, brainstorming, whereby you come up with as many ideas as you can think of without evaluating them until later, is an integral part of the creative process. Later review shows that many of the ideas generated through brainstorming are nonsensical.)

- 'I have to think of something creative straight away.'

(Another integral part of the creative process is patience and, as you might be able to tell, the above rigid belief will lead to impatience. In particular, the person will give up thinking creatively if his first thought is not creative. Indeed, the rigid belief will itself prevent creativity since the person will be involved in evaluating his ideas rather than be fully engaged in the process of open-minded thinking.)

- 'I must know that my ideas will not be laughed at or scorned when I present them.'

(This rigid belief will lead you to play safe by not developing ideas that you think others may well laugh at or scorn. This defensive caution is again the antithesis of creativity which is marked by the development of ideas that may well seem ridiculous at first sight. Also, if you are overly focused on how others may judge your ideas you will not give yourself fully to the creative process. Indeed, a large part of your mind will be on non-creative factors, i.e. the likely response of others.)

Now let me consider the flexible alternatives to these rigid beliefs and consider the beneficial effect of holding such flexible ideas.

- 'It would be good if the creative process were effortless, but it does not have to be that way.'

(If you hold this belief then you assert your desire – effortless creativity – but you importantly go on to acknowledge that this condition does not have to be present for you to engage in the creative process. Holding this flexible belief will also help you to accept that creativity is rarely effortless and may well involve discomfort. This acceptance does not deter you from engaging in the creative process. In fact, it encourages such engagement.)

- 'It would be nice if my ideas made sense to me and/or others, but they do not have to do so.'

(Again, holding this flexible belief allows you to assert your desire – in this case that your ideas make sense – and to acknowledge that this desire does not have to occur. This will enable you to accept that you will have a larger proportion of ideas that will not make sense than ideas that will make sense and that this ratio is an integral part of the creative process.)

- 'It would be good to think of something creative straight away, but it does not have to be that way.'

(This belief would lead you to be more patient and tolerant of the fact that good creative ideas are not as instant as you might like. Just like the gold prospectors of old who were prepared to be patient in their search for actual gold nuggets, this flexible belief encourages you to be patient in your search for creative gold nuggets.)

- 'I would like to know that my ideas will not be laughed at or scorned when I present them, but I do not have to know that and I do not have to be spared such laughter or scorn.'

(This flexible belief will lead you to take sensible risks in developing ideas that you think others may well laugh at or scorn. This lack of defensive caution is an important feature of creativity which, as I have said, is marked by the development of ideas that may well seem ridiculous at first sight. Freed from being overly focused on how others may judge your ideas, you will be able to give yourself fully to the creative process. Albert Ellis (1913–2007), the founder of REBT, introduced this therapy to a largely hostile field in 1955. He resolved to talk and write about REBT at every opportunity despite the fact that his ideas were greeted with much scorn and ridicule. If he had held a rigid belief about being laughed at and scorned, then, in all probability, you would not be reading these words because REBT would not have been developed.)

Working towards flexibility as a goal

Abraham Maslow (1968) once said that self-actualisation cannot be achieved once and for all. It is a state towards which we strive. I agree with this. Albert Ellis (1976) argued that humans have both a tendency to be rational and a tendency to be irrational. We cannot kill off or eliminate our tendency to be irrational. Since flexibility is a major characteristic of rationality and rigidity a major characteristic of irrationality, I would say that if we can work towards increasing the times when we hold flexible beliefs and decreasing the times when we hold rigid beliefs then we are working towards psychological health.

Thus, if in a specific situation you begin by holding a rigid belief, this is not necessarily a sign of psychological disturbance since it is possible for you to stand back and change this belief to its flexible alternative. As will be seen from the next section, engaging in a struggle between being flexible and being rigid is a common feature of psychological health as long as you end up by holding the flexible belief.

A realistic flexibility credo

In this final section, I will outline what I call a realistic flexibility credo. I will put this credo in the first person and as you read it bear in mind that it is a general credo that needs to be applied to specific situations.

As a human being I recognise that I have many desires. I prefer certain conditions to exist in my life and other conditions not to exist. When faced with the possibility of not getting preferred conditions, I tend to demand that these conditions must exist, and faced with the possibility of getting conditions that I don't like, I tend to demand that these must not exist. It is a real struggle for me to acknowledge that no matter how strong my desires are, sadly and regretfully, this does not mean that I have to have my desires met either by myself, by others or by life conditions. In the journey towards believing this, I may well do many things to deal with my disturbed feelings which may help me in the short term, but not in the long term. Thus, I may well deny that I feel disturbed and say either that I am not bothered about what happened or that I am handling it well. However, I recognise that denial is not healthy and I will use it as a cue to think rationally about undesirable conditions as soon as I am able. While I recognise that I can do this, I also acknowledge that there will be times when I won't. The path towards greater flexibility is a rocky one. When I do eventually think flexibly, I will accept that when I don't get my desires met, I will feel badly about this, even though I have acknowledged that I don't have to get what I want. These bad feelings are healthy. They are a sign that I have desires and that these desires are not being met and they motivate me to change things if they can be changed and to adjust constructively if they can't be changed. However, I also recognise that it is very difficult for me to have desires about life conditions and to keep these desires flexible. As such, I will return to disturbed negative feelings when I go back to holding rigid demands.

While flexible beliefs will help me to move towards greater psychological health, I recognise that even when I work hard to develop such beliefs, I will often return to thinking rigidly. Similarly, I acknowledge that as I work to internalise this realistic credo, I will experience many lapses along the way. The best way of dealing with these lapses is to accept them, without liking them, learn specific things from them and act on such specific learning in relevant future situations.

When I acknowledge that holding flexible beliefs is healthy this becomes another preferred condition in my life. As such, I may well demand that I have to think flexibly which paradoxically is evidence that I am in fact thinking rigidly. When this happens, I will again recognise that I have made a rigid dogma out of flexible thinking and will work towards thinking flexibly about flexible thinking by showing myself that while it is desirable for me to think and act in flexible ways, I do not have to do so.

So what are the advantages and disadvantages of a realistic flexibility credo? The advantages seem to be as follows:

1   It gives people a warts-and-all picture of flexibility that is within the grasp of most people.
2   Even though periods of rigid thinking and denial are present in realistic flexibility, there is still a clear indication of the rational thinking that people should aim for.
3   It can comfort rather than inspire and can thus motivate those people who value realism in their quest for greater flexibility.

However, there are disadvantages to the realistic flexibility credo:

1   It may legitimise disturbance and denial as necessary components of flexibility, whereas, in reality, they are frequently rather than inevitably occurring components.
2   It may discourage those people who are capable of a more ideal form of flexibility (i.e. one relatively free from disturbance and denial) from seeing flexibility as a legitimate goal.

However, in my view the advantages of this credo outweigh its disadvantages and, given its realistic nature, it is useful for a person to apply it in dealing flexibly with situations when his or her desires are not met.

In the following three chapters, I will consider three healthy beliefs that stem from the core platform of flexibility: non-awfulising beliefs, discomfort tolerance beliefs and acceptance beliefs. I will begin by discussing non-awfulising.

Chapter 3

Non-awfulising

Introduction

In the previous chapter, I argued that holding flexible beliefs about life's adversities is the foundation of psychological health and that three other rational beliefs are derived from these flexible beliefs. When we hold such beliefs, we:

- hold non-extreme non-awfulising (as opposed to extreme awfulising) beliefs about life's adversities
- believe that we are able to tolerate (as opposed to not tolerate) the discomfort of facing these adversities
- adopt an accepting (as opposed to a depreciating) attitude towards ourselves, other people and life conditions as these relate to the adversities.

In this chapter, I will concentrate on the concept of holding non-awfulising beliefs when we face life's adversities.

The two basic components of non-awfulising beliefs

In this section, I will discuss the two basic components of holding non-awfulising beliefs in the face of life's adversities: an evaluation of badness component and an anti-awfulising component.

The evaluation of badness component of non-awfulising beliefs

When something bad happens to us and we prefer, but do not demand, that this bad event not happen, then we will healthily

evaluate this state of affairs as being bad. This evaluation of badness is the same when your positive preference is not met and when
your negative preference is met.

Evaluations of badness and positive and negative preferences

As I pointed out in the previous chapter, positive preferences
point to what we want to happen and negative preferences point to
what we don't want to happen. Here are some examples of how
evaluations of badness are related to both positive and negative
preferences.

Positive preference unmet and evaluation of badness

- 'I want you to love me and it would be bad if you don't.'
- 'I wanted to do well in my exam and it is unfortunate that I did
  not do so.'

Negative preference met and evaluation of badness

- 'I prefer not to get swine flu and it would be bad if I did get it.'
- 'I prefer not to get a bad report and it would be unfortunate if
  I did get one.'

We differ markedly in the content of our evaluations of badness

In the same way as we differ markedly in the content of our preferences, we also differ markedly in the content of our evaluations of
badness. Thus, some of us think that it is bad when there is an
element of risk present in the things that we do because we prefer
that element to be absent, while others think that it is bad when this
element of risk is absent because we prefer it to be present.

Evaluations of badness vary along a strength continuum

Our evaluations of badness can vary along a continuum of strength
in that we can rate something as mildly bad (e.g. 'It is mildly bad if
I don't beat you at tiddlywinks') or as very strongly bad (e.g. 'It

would be very bad if I was not promoted at work'). The strength of our evaluations of badness is closely related to the strength with which we hold our preferences when they are not met. Thus, when I hold a mild preference for something (e.g. 'I mildly want to beat you at tiddlywinks . . .'), then my evaluation of badness will be mild ('. . . and therefore it will be mildly bad if I lose to you'). However, if I hold a very strong preference for something (e.g. 'I very much want to be promoted at work . . .'), then my evaluation of badness will be correspondingly strong ('. . . and therefore it will be very bad if I am not').

As with strong preferences, it is a defining feature of REBT as a therapeutic approach that when someone is disturbed about an adversity (e.g. the person has failed to be promoted at work) the REBT therapist does not attempt to encourage the person to reduce the strength of his (in this case) evaluation of badness for failing to get promoted. This is because the REBT view of psychological disturbance holds that such disturbance is not a consequence of bad things happening, no matter how strong one's evaluations of badness are. Rather, such disturbance stems from holding awfulising beliefs where extreme evaluations of horror are made. Thus, there is nothing intrinsically disturbing for the person to evaluate an adversity as being very bad. Here, if the therapist attempts to help him to reduce the strength of his evaluation of badness, then the therapist will not help him to address the source of his disturbance. Rather, the therapist will be encouraging the person to lie to himself, to persuade himself that the strength of his evaluation of badness is not as strong as it actually is.

The evaluation of badness component of awfulising beliefs

So far, I have discussed the evaluation of badness component of non-awfulising beliefs. However, this component is also present in awfulising beliefs. Let's again take the case of Erica who I first discussed in Chapter 2. It is very important for her to get a place on a prestigious Ph.D. programme. However, she is also very anxious about the possibility that she may not gain entry into this programme. REBT theory holds that it is not the strength of Erica's non-extreme evaluation of badness that explains her anxiety. This evaluation is stated thus: 'It would be very bad if I do not get onto the Ph.D. programme.' Erica becomes anxious when she transforms her evaluation of badness component into an extreme awfulising belief, thus: 'It would be very bad if I do not get onto the Ph.D. programme and therefore it would be horrible if I fail to do so.' While this extreme belief is usually articulated with the evaluation of badness component omitted (e.g. 'It would be horrible if I don't get onto the Ph.D. programme'), as we have seen, this extreme belief is comprised of a non-extreme evaluation of badness component and an extreme awfulising component.

As noted earlier, a non-awfulising belief is comprised of two components: an evaluation of badness component and an anti-awfulising component. This latter component actively states that the person concerned does not transform the badness component into an extreme evaluation of horror. Thus, if we return to Erica's example, in being helped to develop a non-awfulising belief she was encouraged to maintain the strength of her badness evaluation, but to negate the extreme evaluation of horror. Her new non-awfulising belief was thus: 'It would be very bad if I do not get onto the Ph.D. programme, but not terrible.' This latter component ('. . . but not terrible') is the one that determines Erica's new healthy response of concern about the prospect of not getting onto the Ph.D. programme.

Table 4 makes the point that it is the awfulising component that underpins Erica's feelings of anxiety, while it is the anti-awfulising component that underpins her feelings of concern. This table shows clearly that the evaluation of badness component is the same for both beliefs.

Table 4 Non-awfulising and awfulising beliefs, their components and their emotional consequences

Awfulising belief	Evaluation of badness component	Awfulising component	Emotion
'It would be terrible if I don't get onto the Ph.D. programme'	'It would be bad if I don't get onto the Ph.D. programme . . .	. . . and therefore it would be terrible'	Anxiety
Non-awfulisng belief	Evaluation of badness component	Anti-awfulising component	Emotion
'It would be bad if I don't onto the Ph.D. programme, but not terrible'	'It would be bad if I don't get onto the Ph.D. programme . . .	. . . but not terrible'	Concern

The anti-awfulising component of non-awfulising beliefs

I made the point above that awfulising beliefs and non-awfulising beliefs both contain an evaluation of badness component. Thus, this component does not differentiate between these beliefs. It is the second component that is the important component in helping us to distinguish between these two beliefs.

Understanding the anti-awfulising component of a non-awfulising belief by first understanding the awfulising component of an awfulising belief

One can best understand the anti-awfulising component of a non-extreme non-awfulising belief by first understanding the awfulising component of an extreme awfulising belief. As Table 4 shows, a belief in this domain becomes extreme when the person transforms her (in this case) evaluation of badness component into an extreme awfulising belief. Thus, in her awfulising belief, Erica begins by acknowledging 'It would be bad if I don't get onto the Ph.D. programme . . .' Then she transforms this evaluation of badness component into an awfulising belief by adding the awfulising component: '. . . and therefore it would be terrible'. You will note from Table 4 that an awfulising belief is often expressed with the evaluation of badness component omitted ('It would be terrible if I don't get onto the Ph.D. programme'). This is why I have deconstructed the awfulising belief to show how the person adds the awfulising component to the evaluation of badness component to create her awfulising belief. Thus:

> Evaluation of badness component + Awfulising component
> = Awfulising belief

The nature of an anti-awfulising component

As the name makes clear, the basic nature of an anti-awfulising component of a non-awfulising belief is that it negates horror. Thus, when it is articulated the person needs to make clear that she (in this case) is explicitly stating that horror is not present in the non-awfulising belief. In Erica's case, you will see that she first states the evaluation of badness component of her non-awfulising belief: 'It would be bad if I don't get onto the Ph.D. programme . . .' Then, by adding the anti-awfulising component of her non-awfulising belief ('. . . but not terrible'), she very explicitly states that horror is not present in this belief and it is thus non-extreme. Thus:

Evaluation of badness component + Anti-awfulising component = Non-awfulising belief

---

Here are other examples of anti-awfulising components. These are underlined in the following non-awfulising beliefs:

- 'It is bad if you don't love me, but it is not the end of the world if you don't.'
- 'It is unfortunate if life is not easier for me, but not awful.'

Evaluations of badness: full and part

As with preferences, evaluations of badness can be expressed in their part or full form. The danger of putting an evaluation of badness in its part form is that you can then easily transform it into an extreme awfulising belief, as we will see. Part (or partial) evaluations of badness are shown in the following examples:

- 'It is bad if you don't love me.'
- 'It is unfortunate if life is not easier for me.'

As my analysis of evaluations of badness in this chapter shows, we are not sure if these statements are relative or not. Since part evaluations of badness lack an explicit non-extreme component, the following possibilities exist:

1   A partial evaluation of badness is non-extreme (and thus is equated to a non-awfulising belief) and the non-extreme component is present, but unstated. Here, the person truly believes the following:

- 'It is bad if you don't love me, <u>but it is not the end of the world if you don't.</u>'
- 'It is unfortunate if life is not easier for me, <u>but not awful.</u>'

Please note that in the above beliefs, the unstated components are underlined.

2. A partial evaluation of badness is extreme and the person transforms the partial component into an extreme belief, but does this implicitly without stating that he has done so. Here the person truly believes the following:

- 'It is bad if you don't love me <u>and therefore it is the end of the world if you don't.</u>'
- 'It is unfortunate if life is not easier for me <u>and therefore awful.</u>'

Again, the unstated components are underlined.

Because partial evaluations of badness are so unclear, it is important to express non-awfulising beliefs in their full form (i.e. with both the evaluation of badness component and the anti-awfulising component being clearly stated).

Determining whether a belief is a non-awfulising belief or an awfulising belief

As I mentioned in the previous chapter, when attempting to ascertain whether a person holds a rational belief (in this case a non-extreme non-awfulising belief) or an irrational belief (in this case an extreme awfulising belief), it is important to examine the consequences of such beliefs.

Thus, if the person holds a non-extreme non-awfulising belief, he will tend to experience the following consequences:

- Healthy negative emotions
- Constructive behaviours and action tendencies
- Realistic and balanced subsequent thinking.

And if the person holds an extreme awfulising belief, he will tend to experience:

- Unhealthy negative emotions
- Unconstructive behaviours and action tendencies

- Highly distorted subsequent thinking that is heavily skewed to the negative.

Let me illustrate this by revisiting the cases of Cynthia and Linda whom we met in the previous chapter. If you recall, they were both made redundant from their jobs in the same company on the same day. Their jobs were equally important to them and therefore the loss of their job was equivalent in meaning to both.

Cynthia was depressed about the loss because she believed that it was terrible for her to lose her job. This led her to withdraw into herself and not make any attempt to apply for new jobs. Rather than seek and use support from her family and friends, she claimed things were hopeless and accused people of not being sympathetic whenever they made helpful suggestions. She had the following thoughts: 'I will never get another job so it's not worth trying' and 'I will end up on the scrapheap of life'. These subsequent thoughts are, as can be seen, very skewed to the negative.

Linda, on the other hand, was sad, but not depressed about being made redundant because she believed that it was bad for her to lose her job, but not terrible. This led her to acknowledge and work through her loss, to stay connected with others, to apply for new jobs, and to seek and use support from friends and family members. Needless to say, Linda found a new job quite quickly, whereas Cynthia remained unemployed for much longer. Linda had the following thoughts: 'Getting a job may be difficult, but if I keep trying, I will probably get one' and 'Even if I don't get a job, I can still find meaning and pleasure in life'. These thoughts are realistic and balanced rather than highly distorted and heavily skewed to the negative.

Why non-awfulising beliefs are rational or healthy

In REBT, beliefs are rational or healthy if they meet three criteria:

- They are true.
- They are logical.
- They have healthy consequences.

By these criteria, non-awfulising beliefs are rational or healthy. Let me elaborate.

Non-awfulising beliefs are true

A non-awfulising belief is non-extreme, as is the world; it thus reflects the reality of the way things are. Thus when you are holding a non-awfulising belief you think that whatever you are evaluating is:

(a) Less than 100 per cent bad. Here, you acknowledge that something can always be worse.
(b) As bad as it is, no better, no worse. Here, you may wish that the situation under consideration was not as bad as it is, but you do not demand that it shouldn't be as bad. Also you realise that:
(c) Good can come from this bad event. Here, you appreciate that, in time, some positives may come from this very aversive event and that there are, in all probability, few if any events from which lessons cannot be learned.

When you hold a non-awfulising belief, you do put things into a wider perspective. In doing so, you recognise that when you place the event in a broader time perspective or when you compare it to other aversive events, it is true that the event is bad, but not awful.

Let's look at the proposition that non-awfulising beliefs are true in a different way. As we have seen, a non-awfulising belief has two component parts: (1) an evaluation of badness component (e.g. 'It is bad if I don't do well in my job . . .') and (2) an anti-awfulising component where you negate the idea that what is bad is awful (e.g. '. . . but it is not awful'). Now, you can prove that it is bad if you don't do well; after all you will either not get various things that you want or will get various things that you don't want. Thus, if anyone asks you why it is bad for you not to do well in your job, you can give him or her reasons to prove that it is bad (e.g. it decreases your chances of promotion and of getting a bonus). Furthermore, you can also prove that it is not awful if you don't do well in your job. As discussed above, if it were true that not doing well in your job was awful, nothing could be worse and no good could ever come from this no matter from which perspective you viewed this event. This is obviously not the case because (a) a minute's reflection will enable you to think of several events that could be worse than not doing well in your job, and (b) you could learn from not doing well in your job and improve your performance.

So when you consider the two parts of your non-awfulising belief, (1) 'It is bad if I don't do well in my job . . .' and (2) '. . . but it is not awful', you can see that both parts are true and therefore the belief is true.

Non-awfulising beliefs are logical

As we have seen, all non-awfulising beliefs are also based on an evaluation of badness component. In our example, the non-awfulising belief contains the statement 'It is bad if I don't do well in my job', which is an evaluation of badness component, and the statement 'but it is not awful', which negates the awfulising (and is the anti-awfulising component).

Now if we take the two components of a non-awfulising belief, the evaluation of badness component and the anti-awfulising component, you will see that the latter does follow logically from the former.

The evaluation of badness component is non-extreme and the anti-awfulising component is also non-extreme. It is perfectly logical for two non-extreme components to be linked together. Thus, the statement 'It is bad if I don't do well in my job' does lead logically to the statement 'but it is not awful'. So a non-awfulising belief is logical because it links together two non-extreme statements.

Thus:

> Non-awfulising belief = Evaluation of badness component (non-extreme) + Anti-awfulising component (non-extreme)

e.g. 'It is bad if I don't do well in my job, but it is not awful' (non-awfulising belief) = 'It is bad if I don't do well in my job . . .' (non-extreme, evaluation of badness component) + '. . . but it is not awful' (non-extreme, anti-awfulising component).

The non-awfulising belief is logical because its non-extreme, anti-awfulising component does follow logically from its non-extreme, evaluation of badness component:

> Non-extreme $\longrightarrow$ [logical] $\longrightarrow$ Non-extreme

e.g. 'It is bad if I don't do well in my job . . .' (non-extreme) $\longrightarrow$ [logical] $\longrightarrow$ '. . . but it is not awful' (non-extreme).

Thus, non-awfulising beliefs are logical.

Non-awfulising beliefs are helpful

First, non-awfulising beliefs tend to lead to one or more of the following *healthy* negative emotions when you encounter adversities at 'A': concern, sadness, remorse, disappointment, sorrow, healthy anger, healthy jealousy and healthy envy. Second, non-awfulising beliefs tend to lead to constructive behaviour in the face of adversities such as: facing up to and dealing with difficult situations, sensible working hours, healthy exercise patterns and healthy eating and drinking patterns. Third, non-awfulising beliefs tend to lead to subsequent realistic thinking, such as making realistic estimates of adversities happening, viewing positive events as equally as likely to occur as negative events, seeing negative events in perspective and in a sensible context, and making an objective appraisal of your coping resources.

Holding non-awfulising beliefs leads to similar consequences to those that stem from flexibility

As we have just seen, when you hold a non-awfulising belief when facing an adversity, you will experience a number of emotional, behavioural and cognitive effects that will increase your chances of changing the adversity if it can be changed or of adjusting constructively to it if it cannot be changed. However, there are other positive aspects of holding non-awfulising beliefs and because these beliefs stem from flexibility these positive aspects are the same as those I discussed in the previous chapter (see pp. 19–26). I will summarise these consequences here, but suggest that you refer to pp. 19–26 for an extended discussion of this issue.

Non-awfulising beliefs help you to:

- 'roll with the punches' when hit by an adversity
- adjust to change
- initiate constructive change
- embrace complexity
- be creative.

Working towards holding non-awfulising beliefs as a goal

As I pointed out in the previous chapter, rationality is a state towards which we strive rather than one that can be achieved once and for all. In the same way as we can work towards being more flexible (see Chapter 2), we can also work towards holding non-awfulising beliefs in the face of adversity. If we can work towards increasing the times when we hold non-extreme, non-awfulising beliefs and towards decreasing the times when we hold extreme, awfulising beliefs, then we are working towards psychological health.

Thus, if in a specific situation, you begin by holding an awfulising belief, this is not necessarily a sign of psychological disturbance since it is possible for you to stand back and change this belief to its non-extreme, non-awfulising alternative. As will be seen from the next section, engaging in a struggle between awfulising and non-awfulising is a common feature of psychological health as long as you end up by holding the non-awfulising belief.

Realistic non-awfulising credo

In this final section, I will outline what I call a realistic non-awfulising credo. I will put this credo in the first person and as you read it bear in mind that it is a general credo which needs to be applied to specific situations.

As a human being I recognise that when adversities occur, particularly very bad ones, I may tend to think that it is the end of the world, particularly when I demand that such adversities must not happen. It is a real struggle for me to acknowledge that it is bad, but not awful when these adversities happen. In the journey towards believing this, I may well do many things to deal with my disturbed feelings which may help me in the short term, but not in the long term. Thus, I may well deny that I feel disturbed and say either that I am not bothered about what happened or that I am handling it well. However, I recognise that denial is not healthy and will use this as a cue to think rationally about undesirable conditions as soon as I am able. While I recognise that I can do this, I also acknowledge that there will be times when I won't. The path towards holding non-awfulising beliefs is a rocky one. When I do eventually think in this non-extreme, non-awfulising way, I will accept that when adversities happen, I will feel badly about this, even though I have acknowledged that it is bad, but not awful when these negative events occur. These bad feelings are healthy. They are a sign that negative events have happened and they motivate me to change things if they can be changed and to adjust constructively if they can't be changed. But I also recognise that it is very difficult for me to hold non-awfulising beliefs about adversities and to keep these beliefs non-extreme. As such, I will return to disturbed negative feelings when I go back to holding extreme awfulising beliefs.

While non-awfulising beliefs will help me to move towards greater psychological health, I recognise that even when I work hard to develop such beliefs, I will often return to thinking in an awfulising manner. Similarly, I acknowledge that as I work to internalise this realistic credo, I will experience many lapses along the way. The best way of dealing with these lapses is to accept them, without liking them, learn specific things from them and act on such specific learning in relevant future situations.

When I acknowledge that holding non-awfulising beliefs is healthy this becomes another positive in my life. As such, I may well think that it is awful if I do not think in this non-extreme way, which paradoxically is evidence that I am in fact thinking in an extreme awfulising manner. When this happens, I will again recognise that I have made a horror out of holding an awfulising belief and will work towards thinking in a non-extreme, non-awfulising way about my awfulising beliefs by showing myself that while it is bad for me to think and act in extreme awfulising ways, it is not terrible if I do so.

So what are the advantages and disadvantages of a realistic non-awfulising credo? They are similar to those of the realistic flexibility credo I discussed in Chapter 2. The advantages seem to be as follows:

1   It gives people a warts-and-all picture of non-awfulising thinking that is within the grasp of most people.

2   Even though periods of awfulising thinking and denial are present in realistic non-awfulising, there is still a clear indication of the rational thinking that people should aim for.
3   It can comfort rather than inspire and can thus motivate those people who value realism in their quest for greater non-awfulising.

However, there are disadvantages to the realistic non-awfulising credo, as there are with the realistic flexibility credo:

1   It may legitimise disturbance and denial as necessary components of non-awfulising, whereas, in reality, they are frequently rather than inevitably occurring components.
2   It may discourage those people who are capable of a more ideal form of non-awfulising (i.e. one relatively free from disturbance and denial) from seeing non-awfulising as a legitimate goal.

However, in my view the advantages of this credo outweigh its disadvantages and, given its realistic nature, it is useful for a person to apply it when striving to hold non-awfulising beliefs about adversities.

In the following chapter, I discuss the healthy concept of discomfort tolerance.

Chapter 4

Discomfort tolerance

Introduction

Believing that we are able to tolerate (as opposed to not tolerate) the discomfort of facing adversities is a key ingredient of psychological health. As used here discomfort is a generic term which points to a negative felt sense that we experience when such adversities happen to us and to those whom we care about. Such discomfort may be acute or it may be chronic. It may involve the pain when we get what we don't want or the displeasure of being deprived of what we do want.

Our perceived ability to tolerate discomfort can be regarded as just that: our view concerning whether or not we are able to put up with such discomfort. However, discomfort tolerance needs to be viewed more broadly and is best allied with two ideas. The first allied idea is this: 'Is it worth it to me to tolerate such discomfort?' And the second idea is: 'Am I worth tolerating discomfort for?' I will discuss these ideas later in the chapter.

The three basic components of discomfort tolerance beliefs

In this section, I will discuss the three basic components of holding discomfort tolerance beliefs in the face of life's adversities: a struggle component, a toleration component and a 'worth it' component.

The struggle component of discomfort tolerance beliefs

When something bad happens to us and we prefer, but do not demand, that this bad event not happen, then we will tend to think that we can tolerate the ensuing discomfort even though doing so will be a struggle. The latter part of this belief as stated here emphasises that discomfort tolerance is not an effortless enterprise. It involves a real struggle, particularly when the felt sense of the discomfort is highly aversive. This struggle is the same when your positive preference is not met (i.e. you don't get what you want) and when your negative preference is met (i.e. you get what you don't want).

Struggle and positive and negative preferences

As I pointed out in Chapter 2, positive preferences point to what we want to happen and negative preferences point to what we don't want to happen. Here are some examples of how struggle is related to both positive and negative preferences.

Positive preferences unmet and struggle

- 'I want you to love me and it would be difficult for me to put up with if you don't.'
- 'I wanted to do well in my exam and it is hard for me to tolerate the fact that I did not do so.'

Negative preferences met and struggle

- 'I prefer not to get swine flu and it would hard to stand if I did get it.'
- 'I prefer not to get a bad report and it would be a struggle for me to tolerate it if I did not get one.'

We differ markedly in the content of our struggles

In the same way as we differ markedly in the content of our preferences, we also differ markedly in the content of our struggles. Thus, some of us think that it is difficult to tolerate when there is an element of risk present in the things that we do because we prefer that element to be absent, while others think that it is difficult to tolerate when this element of risk is absent because we prefer it to be present.

Struggle and the intensity and type of discomfort

When we think of struggle and discomfort, it is important to consider the intensity and type of discomfort experienced.

Struggle and the intensity of discomfort

Some people find it difficult to put up with even mild forms of discomfort ('It is difficult for me to put up with discomfort of any kind'), while others only struggle when such discomfort is intense and can easily tolerate milder forms of discomfort (e.g. 'When I feel very uncomfortable, I find it very difficult to tolerate this'). People in the former group can be said to be discomfort averse and they easily transform their struggles into discomfort intolerance beliefs (e.g. 'Because I find it very difficult to put up with any form of discomfort, this means that I can't put up with it'). They are much more likely to abuse a range of substances in their quest to avoid discomfort, particularly when they have transformed their struggles into discomfort tolerance beliefs as in the example just provided. Indeed, they are so discomfort averse that they think that any discomfort that they will experience will be more intense than it actually will be. The therapeutic task with such people is to encourage them to increase their discomfort tolerance gradually and to help them see that their predictions of the intensity of future discomfort are generally inaccurate. When they do face up to discomfort and stay in the situation without resorting to ways of dodging discomfort, they generally find that the intensity of discomfort drops over time.

People in the latter group are not generally discomfort averse and only really struggle when they encounter intense discomfort. Their predictions of discomfort intensity tend to be more accurate than those made by people who are generally discomfort averse.

Struggle and the type of discomfort

There are different types of discomfort and just because you may struggle with one type does not mean that you will struggle with all types. For example, the discomfort you will experience when you need to move from a comfortable state to an uncomfortable state will be different from the discomfort you will experience when you are faced with temptation and want to refrain from engaging in whatever it is that tempts you. Let me illustrate this point with the case of Kevin. Every morning Kevin chooses to get up at 6.30 to go jogging before work, whatever the weather. This involves him facing the discomfort of leaving his nice warm bed to go out to run, often in the cold. Kevin does this without much of a struggle. However, Kevin experiences far more of a struggle not eating savoury snacks when they are offered to him. The first form of discomfort comes from making a transition from a comfortable state (i.e. lying in bed) to an uncomfortable state (i.e. getting up to run), while the second type comes from being in a deprived state, where Kevin struggles not to act on an urge to engage in pleasurable, but self-undisciplined behaviour (see Chapter 7).

There is also a difference between acute discomfort and chronic discomfort. People generally struggle more with acute discomfort than with chronic discomfort. Indeed, people will often put up with chronic discomfort to avoid the more acute discomfort that change will lead to.

The struggle component of discomfort intolerance beliefs

So far, I have discussed the struggle component of a discomfort tolerance belief. However, this component is also present in discomfort intolerance. Let's again take the case of Erica whom I first discussed in Chapter 2. It is very important for her to get a place on a prestigious Ph.D. programme. However, she is also very anxious about the possibility that she may not gain entry onto this programme. REBT theory holds that it is not the strength of Erica's non-extreme struggle component that explains her anxiety. This component is stated thus: 'It would be very hard for me to tolerate it if I do not get onto the Ph.D. programme.' Erica becomes anxious when she transforms her struggle component into an extreme discomfort intolerance belief, thus: 'It would be very hard for me to tolerate it if I do not get onto the Ph.D. programme and therefore I could not bear it if I fail to do so.' While this extreme belief is usually articulated with the struggle component omitted (e.g. 'I could not bear it if I don't get onto the Ph.D. programme'), as we have seen, this extreme belief is comprised of both a struggle component and an extreme 'it's intolerable' component.

As noted earlier, a discomfort tolerance belief is comprised of three components: a struggle component, a toleration component and a 'worth it' component. The second of these three components actively states that the person concerned does not transform the struggle component into an extreme 'it's intolerable' belief. Thus, if we return to Erica's example, in being helped to develop a discomfort tolerance belief, she was encouraged to maintain the strength of her struggle component, but to negate the extreme 'it's intolerable' component. She was also helped to see that it was worth it to her to put up with not getting onto the Ph.D. programme. Her new discomfort tolerance belief was thus: 'It would be a great struggle for me if I do not get onto the Ph.D. programme, but I could tolerate not doing so and it is worth it to me to do so.' The second component ('. . . but I could tolerate not doing so') is the one that determines Erica's new healthy response of concern about the prospect of not getting onto the Ph.D. programme.

Table 5 makes the point that it is the intolerance component that underpins Erica's feelings of anxiety, while it is the toleration and 'worth it' components that underpin her feelings of concern. This table shows clearly that the struggle component is the same for both beliefs.

Table 5 Discomfort tolerance and discomfort intolerance beliefs, their components and their emotional consequences

Discomfort intolerance belief	Struggle component	Intolerance component		Emotion
'I could not tolerate it if I don't get onto the Ph.D. programme'	'It would be a great struggle for me if I don't get onto the Ph.D. programme . . .	. . . and therefore I could not tolerate it'		Anxiety
Discomfort tolerance belief	Struggle component	Toleration component	'Worth it' component	Emotion
'It would be a great struggle for me if I don't get onto the Ph.D. programme, but I could tolerate not doing so and it is worth it to me to do so'	'It would be a great struggle for me if I don't get onto the Ph.D. programme . . .	. . . but I could tolerate not doing so . . .	. . . and it is worth it to me to do so'	Concern

The toleration component of discomfort tolerance beliefs

I made the point above that discomfort intolerance beliefs and discomfort tolerance beliefs both contain a sense of struggle. Thus, this component does not differentiate between these beliefs. It is the second and third components that are the important components in helping us to distinguish between these two beliefs.

Understanding the toleration component of a discomfort tolerance belief by first understanding the intolerance component of a discomfort intolerance belief

One can best understand the toleration component of a non-extreme discomfort tolerance belief by first understanding the intolerance component of an extreme discomfort intolerance belief. As Table 5 shows, a belief in this domain becomes extreme when the person transforms her (in this case) struggle component into an extreme discomfort intolerance belief. Thus, in her discomfort intolerance belief, Erica begins by acknowledging 'It would be a great struggle for me if I do not get onto the Ph.D. programme . . .' Then she transforms this struggle component into a discomfort intolerance belief by adding the intolerance component: '. . . and therefore I could not tolerate it'. You will note from Table 5 that a discomfort intolerance belief is often expressed with the struggle component omitted ('I could not tolerate it if I don't get onto the Ph.D. programme'). This is why I have deconstructed the discomfort intolerance belief to show how the person adds the intolerance component to the struggle component to create her discomfort intolerance belief. Thus:

> Struggle component + Intolerance component = Discomfort intolerance belief

The nature of a toleration component

As the name makes clear, the basic nature of a toleration component of a discomfort tolerance belief is that it negates the idea of intolerance. Thus, when it is articulated, the person makes clear that she (in this case) is explicitly stating that intolerance is not present in the discomfort tolerance belief. In Erica's case, you will see that she first states the struggle component of her discomfort tolerance belief: 'It would be a great struggle for me if I do not get onto the Ph.D. programme . . .' Then, by adding the toleration component of her discomfort tolerance belief ('. . . but I could tolerate not doing so . . .'), she very explicitly states that intolerance is not present in this belief and it is thus non-extreme. Thus:

Struggle component + Toleration component + One other component = Discomfort tolerance belief

---

You will notice that there is a third, as yet unspecified, component that needs to be present in a discomfort tolerance belief. This is the 'worth it' component which I will discuss presently.

But first, here are other examples of toleration components. These are underlined in the following discomfort tolerance beliefs:

- 'It is hard to tolerate you not loving me, <u>but I can tolerate it if you don't</u>.' ('worth it' component unspecified as yet)
- 'It is a struggle if life is not easier for me, <u>but I can put up with it</u>.' ('worth it' component unspecified as yet)

Struggle: full and part

As with preferences and evaluations of badness a sense of struggle can be expressed in its part or full form. The danger of expressing struggle in its part form is that you can then easily transform it into an extreme discomfort intolerance belief, as we will see. Part (or partial) struggle beliefs are shown in the following examples:

- 'It is difficult for me to tolerate it if you don't love me.'
- 'It is a struggle putting up with life not being easier for me.'

As my analysis of struggle in this chapter shows, we are not sure if these statements are relative or not. Since part struggle beliefs lack an explicit non-extreme component, the following possibilities exist:

1   The part struggle belief is, in fact, non-extreme (and thus is equated to a discomfort tolerance belief) and the non-extreme component is present, but unstated. Here, the person truly believes the following:

- 'It is difficult for me to tolerate it if you don't love me, <u>but I can do so.</u>'
- 'It is a struggle putting up with life not being easier for me, <u>but I can put up with it.</u>'

Please note that in the above beliefs, the unstated components are underlined.

2   The part struggle belief is extreme and the person transforms the partial component into an extreme belief, but does this implicitly without stating that he has done so. Here the person truly believes the following:

- 'It is difficult for me to tolerate it if you don't love me <u>and, in fact, I cannot do so.</u>'
- 'It is a struggle putting up with life not being easier for me, <u>and I can't put up with it.</u>'

Again, note that the unstated components have been underlined.

Because partial struggle beliefs are so unclear, it is important to express discomfort tolerance beliefs with the struggle component and the toleration component clearly stated and, as I will presently show you, also with the 'worth it' component made explicit.

The 'worth it' component of discomfort tolerance beliefs

As I pointed out earlier in this chapter, there are three components of a discomfort tolerance belief, as opposed to the two components of a discomfort intolerance belief. So far, I have discussed the 'struggle' and 'toleration' components of a discomfort tolerance belief. These components show that while it is a struggle for you to put up with an adversity, it is possible for you to do so. The 'worth it' component adds an important motivational dimension to a discomfort tolerance belief. Thus, here you are acknowledging that while it is not only possible for you to put up with an adversity, albeit with a struggle, it is also worth it (meaning that it is in your healthy best interests) for you to do so.

Let me illustrate this by providing you with a silly example. Let's suppose that I ask you to stand outside your house overnight in a big bowl of cold custard. Would you be able to do this? The answer would be 'yes'. Would it be a struggle for you to do so? Undoubtedly. But would you do it? You would do it if you saw that there was a good reason to do so. Thus, let's suppose that I asked you to do this for 1p. Would you do it? Probably not. However, let's suppose that someone kidnapped a loved one of yours and would only release that person if you agreed to stand outside your house all night in a big bowl of cold custard. Would you do so now? The answer would be 'yes', if you were sure that the kidnapper would keep their end of the bargain and release your loved one.

This shows the importance of the 'worth it' component of discomfort tolerance beliefs. For there are probably many adversities that you could theoretically tolerate, but you would only choose to do so if you clearly saw that it would be in your best interests to tolerate such adversities. By bringing the motivational aspect of a discomfort tolerance belief to the fore, the 'worth it' component transforms the theoretical possibility of tolerating discomfort into the practical reality of doing so.

As mentioned at the beginning of the chapter, you also need to ask yourself: 'Am I worth tolerating this discomfort for?' Many people are prepared to tolerate discomfort if doing so benefits their loved ones, but will not do so for themselves because they do not think that they are worth tolerating the discomfort for. Many people will not go through the arduous business of daily exercise and keeping to a healthy diet for themselves whereas they might do so because a loved one is distressed at the thought of losing them to a heart attack. I will deal with the issue of self-worth in the following chapter. In short, the more you think you are worth tolerating discomfort for, the more you will think that you can tolerate it and the more likely it is that you will tolerate it.

So, in short, when thinking of discomfort tolerance, you need to answer three questions:

- Can I tolerate it?
- Is it worth tolerating?
- Am I worth tolerating it for?

Determining whether a belief is a discomfort tolerance belief or a discomfort intolerance belief

As I have mentioned in the previous two chapters, when attempting to ascertain whether a person holds a rational belief (in this case, a non-extreme discomfort tolerance belief) or an irrational belief (in this case, an extreme discomfort intolerance belief), it is important to examine the consequences of such beliefs.

Thus, if the person holds a non-extreme discomfort tolerance belief, he will tend to experience the following consequences:

- Healthy negative emotions
- Constructive behaviours and action tendencies
- Realistic and balanced subsequent thinking.

And if the person holds an extreme discomfort intolerance belief, he will tend to experience:

- Unhealthy negative emotions
- Unconstructive behaviours and action tendencies
- Highly distorted subsequent thinking that is heavily skewed to the negative.

Let me illustrate this by revisiting the cases of Cynthia and Linda whom we met in the previous two chapters. If you recall, they were both made redundant from their jobs in the same company on the same day. Their jobs were equally important to them and therefore the loss of their job was equivalent in meaning to both.

Cynthia was depressed about the loss because she believed that she could not bear to lose her job. This led her to experience the same consequences as she did when holding a rigid belief and an awfulising belief about the job loss. Thus, she withdrew into herself and did not make any attempt to apply for new jobs. Rather than seek and use support from her family and friends, she claimed things were hopeless and accused people of not being sympathetic whenever they made helpful suggestions. She had the following thoughts: 'I will never get another job so it's not worth trying' and 'I will never recover from this'. These subsequent thoughts are, as can be seen, highly distorted and very skewed to the negative.

Linda, on the other hand, was sad, but not depressed about being made redundant because she believed that while it was a struggle for her to tolerate losing her job, she could tolerate it and it was worth her while to do so. As with her flexible and non-awfulising beliefs, this discomfort tolerance belief led her to acknowledge and work through her loss, to stay connected with others, to apply for new jobs, and to seek and use support from friends and family members. Needless to say, Linda found a new job quite quickly, whereas Cynthia remained unemployed for much longer. Linda had the following thoughts: 'Getting a job may be difficult, but if I keep trying, I will probably get one' and 'Even if I don't get a job, I will recover from the loss and can still find meaning and pleasure in life'. These thoughts are realistic and balanced rather than highly distorted and heavily skewed to the negative.

Why discomfort tolerance beliefs are rational or healthy

We have seen that in REBT, beliefs are rational or healthy if they meet three criteria:

- They are true.
- They are logical.
- They have healthy consequences.

By these criteria, discomfort tolerance beliefs are rational or healthy. Let me elaborate.

Discomfort tolerance beliefs are true

A discomfort tolerance belief points to your perceived ability to tolerate adversities. It tends to be true because your ability to tolerate adversities is such that you can withstand and transcend all manner of traumas, tragedies and catastrophes. Discomfort tolerance means one or more of the following:

(a) Virtually all adversities (especially highly aversive ones) are difficult to tolerate, but they can be tolerated. Therefore, you will neither die nor disintegrate if you encounter such events.

(b) You may find it difficult to feel happy in the face of adversities, but this does not mean that you have lost the capacity for happiness.

When you hold a discomfort tolerance belief, you are able to adopt a longer-term perspective and can see a future. As such, you are able to consider that whatever it is that you are finding difficult to tolerate is not only tolerable, but is worth tolerating.

Let's look at the proposition that discomfort tolerance beliefs are true in a different way. As I have already mentioned, a discomfort tolerance belief has three components: (1) the first part states what is hard to tolerate (e.g. 'It would be hard to tolerate if I don't do well in my job . . .'); (2) the second part negates the idea that what is hard to tolerate is intolerable (e.g. '. . . but I could tolerate it'), and (3) the third part asserts the reasons for the second part (e.g. '. . . and it is worth it to me to do so').

First, you can prove that not doing well in your job is hard to tolerate; after all you will struggle if you don't do well. Thus, if anyone asks you why not doing well in your job is hard to tolerate, you can give them reasons to prove that it is difficult (e.g. you may have to put in more work to make up for your poor performance, you may have to learn new skills that you don't want to learn or are difficult for you to learn, and you may have your pay reduced so that it would be more of a struggle to make ends meet).

Second, you can also prove that failing to do well in your job is not intolerable. As discussed above, if it were true that not doing well in your job was intolerable, you would die or disintegrate or lose your capacity to experience happiness. None of these are likely to be true, as a moment's reflection will make clear. Indeed, you can show quite clearly that you won't die, disintegrate or lose your capacity to be happy, for you would gladly face the prospect of not doing well in your job to save the life of any of your loved ones. If it were true that you could not tolerate failing to do well in your job, then you would be far less likely to be willing to face this event under these circumstances.

Third, you can provide reasons why it is healthy for you to put up with not doing well in your job. Thus, you can say that tolerating your poor performance will increase the likelihood that you will focus on and address effectively the reasons for your poor performance.

So when you consider the three components of your discomfort tolerance belief – (1) 'It is hard to tolerate not doing well in my job . . .'; (2) '. . . but I could tolerate it and . . .'; (3) '. . . it is worth it to me to do so' – you can see that all parts are true and therefore the discomfort tolerance belief is true.

Discomfort tolerance beliefs are logical

When considering whether or not a discomfort tolerance belief is logical, we need to consider the first two components. In our example, in the discomfort tolerance belief, we have the statement 'It is difficult for me to tolerate not doing well in my job', which is the struggle component, and the statement 'but I could tolerate it', which is the anti-intolerance component.

Now, taking these two components, you will see that the latter does follow logically from the former. The struggle component is non-extreme and the anti-intolerance component is also non-extreme. It is perfectly logical for two non-extreme components to be linked together. Thus, the statement 'It is difficult for me to tolerate not doing well in my job' does lead logically to the statement 'but I could tolerate it'. So a discomfort tolerance belief is logical because it links together two non-extreme statements. Thus:

Discomfort tolerance belief = Struggle component (non-extreme) + Anti-intolerance component (non-extreme)

e.g. 'It is difficult for me to tolerate not doing well in my job . . .' (non-extreme, struggle component) + '. . . but I could tolerate it' (non-extreme, ant-intolerance component).

The discomfort tolerance belief is logical because its non-extreme, anti-intolerance component does follow logically from its non-extreme, struggle component:

Non-extreme $\longrightarrow$ [logical] $\longrightarrow$ Non-extreme

e.g. 'It is difficult for me to tolerate not doing well in my job . . .' (non-extreme) $\longrightarrow$ [logical] $\longrightarrow$ '. . . but I could tolerate it' (non-extreme).

Thus, discomfort tolerance beliefs are logical.

Discomfort tolerance beliefs are helpful

First, discomfort tolerance beliefs tend to lead to one or more of the following healthy negative emotions when you encounter adversities: concern, sadness, remorse, disappointment, sorrow, healthy anger, healthy jealousy and healthy envy. Second, discomfort tolerance beliefs tend to lead to constructive behaviour in the face of negative activating events such as: facing up to and dealing with difficult situations, sensible working hours, healthy exercise patterns and healthy eating and drinking patterns. Third, discomfort tolerance beliefs tend to lead to subsequent realistic thinking, such as making realistic estimates of adversities happening, viewing positive events as equally likely to occur as negative events, seeing negative events in perspective and in a sensible context, and making an objective appraisal of your coping resources.

Finally, while there are many things that you can tolerate that are not worth tolerating, discomfort tolerance beliefs not only stress that you can tolerate the event in question, but also underscore that it is worth it to you to tolerate it. In other words, discomfort tolerance beliefs encourage you to see that it is in your best interests to tolerate such an event and that doing so will help you to achieve your goals.

Holding discomfort tolerance beliefs leads to similar consequences to those that stem from flexible and non-awfulising beliefs

As we have just seen, when you hold a discomfort tolerance belief when facing an adversity, you will experience a number of emotional, behavioural and cognitive effects that will increase your chances of changing the adversity if it can be changed or of adjusting constructively to it if it cannot be changed. However, there are other positive aspects of holding discomfort tolerance beliefs and because these beliefs stem from flexible beliefs these positive aspects are the same as those I discussed in Chapter 2 (see pp. 19–26). I will summarise these consequences here, but suggest that you refer to pp. 19–26 for an extended discussion of this issue.

Discomfort tolerance beliefs help you to:

- 'roll with the punches' when hit by an adversity
- adjust to change

- initiate constructive change
- embrace complexity
- be creative.

Working towards holding discomfort tolerance beliefs as a goal

As I pointed out in Chapter 2, rationality is a state towards which we strive rather than a state that can be achieved once and for all. In the same way as we can work towards being more flexible (see Chapter 2) and towards holding non-awfulising beliefs in the face of adversity (see Chapter 3), we can also work towards holding discomfort tolerance beliefs under such circumstances. If we can work towards increasing the times when we hold non-extreme, discomfort tolerance beliefs and towards decreasing the times when we hold extreme, discomfort intolerance beliefs, then we are working towards psychological health.

Thus, if in a specific situation you begin by holding a discomfort intolerance belief, this is not necessarily a sign of psychological disturbance since it is possible for you to stand back and change this belief to its non-extreme, discomfort tolerance alternative. As will be seen from the next section, engaging in a struggle between holding a discomfort intolerance belief and a discomfort tolerance belief is a common feature of psychological health as long as you end up by holding the discomfort tolerance belief.

A realistic discomfort tolerance credo

In this final section, I will outline what I call a realistic discomfort tolerance credo. I will put this credo in the first person and as you read it bear in mind that it is a general credo which needs to be applied to specific situations.

> As a human being I recognise that when adversities occur, particularly very bad ones, I may tend to think that I can't stand them, particularly when I demand that such adversities must not happen. It is a real struggle for me to put up with these adversities, but I can do so. In the journey towards believing this, I may well do many things

to deal with my disturbed feelings which may help me in the short term, but not in the long term. Thus, I may deny that I feel disturbed and say either that I am not bothered about what happened or that I am handling it well. However, I recognise that denial is not healthy and will use this as a cue to think rationally about undesirable conditions as soon as I am able. While I recognise that I can do this, I also acknowledge that there will be times when I won't. The path towards holding discomfort tolerance beliefs is a rocky one. When I do eventually think in this non-extreme, discomfort tolerance way, I will accept that when adversities happen, I will feel badly about this, even though I have accepted that I can tolerate these events and it is worth it to me to do so. These bad feelings are healthy. They are a sign that negative events have happened and they motivate me to change things if they can be changed and to adjust constructively if they can't be changed. However, I also recognise that it is very difficult for me to hold discomfort tolerance beliefs about adversities and to keep these beliefs non-extreme. As such, I will return to disturbed negative feelings when I go back to holding extreme discomfort intolerance beliefs.

While discomfort tolerance beliefs will help me to move towards greater psychological health, I recognise that even when I work hard to develop such beliefs, I will often return to thinking in a discomfort intolerance manner. Similarly, I acknowledge that as I work to internalise this realistic credo, I will experience many lapses along the way. The best way of dealing with these lapses is to accept them, without liking them, learn specific things from them and act on such specific learning in relevant future situations.

When I acknowledge that holding discomfort intolerance beliefs is healthy this becomes another positive in my life. As such, I may well think that I cannot bear it if I do not think in this non-extreme way, which paradoxically is evidence that I am in fact thinking in an extreme discomfort intolerance manner. When this happens, I will recognise that I am being intolerant about holding a discomfort intolerance belief and will work toward thinking in a more tolerant way about my discomfort intolerance beliefs. I will do this by showing myself that while it is a struggle for me to put up with thinking and acting in extreme discomfort intolerance ways, it is not intolerable if I do so. I can stand this and it is worth it to me to do so since this will help me to get back on the path towards greater discomfort tolerance.

So what are the advantages and disadvantages of a realistic discomfort tolerance credo? They are similar to those of the realistic flexibility and non-awfulising credos that I discussed in Chapters 2 and 3. The advantages seem to be as follows:

1   It gives people a warts-and-all picture of discomfort tolerance thinking that is within the grasp of most people.
2   Even though periods of discomfort intolerance thinking and denial are present in realistic discomfort tolerance, there is still a clear indication of the rational thinking that people should aim for.
3   It can comfort rather than inspire and can thus motivate those people who value realism in their quest for greater discomfort tolerance.

However, there are disadvantages to the realistic discomfort tolerance credo, as there are with the realistic flexibility credo and the realistic non-awfulising credo:

1   It may legitimise disturbance and denial as necessary components of discomfort tolerance, whereas, in reality, they are frequently rather than inevitably occurring components.
2   It may discourage those people who are capable of a more ideal form of discomfort tolerance (i.e. one relatively free from disturbance and denial) from seeing discomfort tolerance as a legitimate goal.

However, in my view the advantages of this credo outweigh its disadvantages and, given its realistic nature, it is useful for a person to apply it when striving to hold discomfort tolerance beliefs about adversities.

In the next chapter, I will discuss acceptance in its three major forms: unconditional life-acceptance, unconditional self-acceptance and unconditional other-acceptance.

Chapter 5

Acceptance

Introduction

In this chapter, I consider the concept of acceptance as it pertains to holding a healthy attitude about adversity. I made the point in Chapter 2 that at the very heart of a psychologically healthy response to adversity is flexibility. I also stated in that chapter that three healthy beliefs stem from the philosophy of flexibility. These are non-awfulising beliefs (discussed in Chapter 3), discomfort tolerance beliefs (discussed in Chapter 4) and acceptance beliefs (which is the focus of the current chapter).

Negative connotations of the term 'acceptance'

Before I discuss the REBT view of acceptance, I want to make the point that people bring to the term 'acceptance' their own sense of what this word means. If you bring a negative connotation to the term, then you will resist acquiring an acceptance belief. Here is a list of connotations of the term 'acceptance' which may impact negatively on the person working to acquire an acceptance belief:

- Accepting an adversity means finding it acceptable.

Here, if you are being encouraged to accept an adversity and you think that you are, in fact, being encouraged to think of the adversity as 'acceptable', then you will resist this effort.

- Accepting an adversity means condoning it.

If you think that by accepting a negative event you are condoning it, then you will not want to accept it.

• Accepting an adversity means resigning yourself to it.

Many people think that acceptance means resigning yourself to something that may or may not be able to be changed. Particularly, when you think that accepting an adversity that could be changed means resigning yourself to it, then you will resist accepting it.

• Accepting an adversity means giving your consent to it.

Consent is a synonym of the word 'approval'. Thus, if you think that accepting an adversity means consenting to it or giving one's approval, then you will not wish to accept it.

Since the term 'acceptance' gives rise to a variety of connotations, it is important that I make explicit how I shall be using the term in three areas:

1   Unconditional life-acceptance (ULA)
2   Unconditional self-acceptance (USA)
3   Unconditional other-acceptance (UOA)

Let me outline what I mean by acceptance in reference to these three areas.

Unconditional life-acceptance I: In the presence of a negative aspect of life

As we will see, accepting life unconditionally involves acknowledging the fact that life is very complex and incorporates positive, negative and neutral aspects of self, others and environmental conditions. I will deal with unconditional life-acceptance in two ways: (a) when you are facing the presence of a negative aspect of life, and (b) when you are facing the absence of a positive aspect of life. I will begin with the former.

In explaining what I mean by accepting life in the presence of a negative aspect of life, I will illustrate my points by referring to a situation where a piece of work that you have done has been criticised by your boss unfairly.

When you accept life in the presence of a negative aspect of life you do the following.

You acknowledge both the presence of the negative aspect and the fact that you don't like its presence

In our example you think:

> 'I acknowledge that my boss has criticised my work unfairly and I really do not like this.'

You hold a flexible belief about the presence of the negative aspect

As I discussed in Chapter 2, holding a flexible belief in this context means that you assert your preference that a negative aspect is not present, but you do not demand that it must not be present. Thus, in our example, you think:

> 'I wish that my boss did not criticise my work unfairly, but sadly he does not have to act according to my wishes.'

You recognise that all the conditions are or were in place for the negative aspect to be present and therefore you acknowledge that it 'should' empirically be present

If you take two parts of hydrogen and add them to one part of oxygen you will get water. This is the case no matter what your feelings are about the matter. Thus, we can say that when these elements are mixed you should empirically get water. All this is saying is that reality when it exists should empirically exist because all the conditions are in place for it to be reality.

Applying this principle to our example, you think:

> 'I know that my boss tends to find fault in things and that he was looking at my work from this perspective. If that is the way he operates, then he should have infairly criticised my work.'

You do not depreciate life for the presence of the negative aspect

Here you acknowledge that it is not possible to evaluate life globally when you don't get what you want because life is far too complex to warrant such a global rating.

'Life is not bad for allowing my boss to criticise my work unfairly.'

You assert the facts about life

Here, while focusing on the negative aspect you assert that life is a complex mixture of positive, negative and neutral aspects.

'While it is bad that my boss criticised my work unfairly, life is a complex mixture of the good, the bad and the neutral and this fact does not change even if my boss may change at some point and stop criticising me.'

This point demonstrates the unconditional nature of unconditional life-acceptance in that life is seen to be unchanged whether the negative aspect is present or not.

You attempt to change the negative aspect if it can be changed and if the benefits outweigh the costs of doing so

This principle asserts that an important part of acceptance is attempting to change negative aspects of life. Acceptance in REBT, therefore, is the antithesis of resignation. Note the placing of this change principle. It appears after the previous two principles because in REBT we argue that changing an adversity is best done when you are not in a disturbed frame of mind. Thus, were you to depreciate life, your attempts to change the negative aspect would be hampered by your disturbance-creating life-depreciation belief. Refusing to depreciate life and asserting the facts of life puts you in a healthy and realistic frame of mind which maximises your chances of effecting change.

In our example, you may speak to your boss, put things to him from your perspective and encourage him to see matters from your frame of reference.

However, even if it is possible to change your boss, you will only decide to do so if the perceived benefits of doing so outweigh the perceived costs. Thus, if your boss is the kind of person to make life more difficult for you if you assert yourself with him, you may decide that it is not in your longer-term healthy interest to raise the issue with him.

You hold a flexible belief about the outcome of
your attempts to change the negative aspect

Here, you want a good outcome from your attempts to change the
negative aspect, but you do not demand that you must be successful in this regard. In our example, you think: 'I want my boss to see
things from my point of view, but he does not have to do so.'

If you cannot change the negative aspect or you
recognise that it is not worth trying to change it,
you acknowledge that this is the case, recognise
that you don't like this, but also recognise that
you can move on with your life without being
preoccupied with the continuing presence of the
negative aspect

If your attempts to change the negative aspect are unsuccessful,
acceptance means acknowledging that you don't like this, but
resolving to move on in your life without being preoccupied with
the continuing presence of the negative aspect. Thus, in our
example, if having heard what you have to say your boss holds to
his position and continues to criticise your work, in your view,
unfairly, then you acknowledge that you don't like this, but that
you can get on with your job despite this fact.

Unconditional life-acceptance II: In the absence of a positive aspect of life

In explaining what I mean by accepting life in the absence of a
positive aspect of life, I will illustrate my points by referring to a
situation where your partner did not remember your birthday.

When you accept life in the absence of a positive aspect of life
you do the following.

You acknowledge both the absence of the positive
aspect and the fact that you don't like its absence

In our example you think:

'I acknowledge that my partner forgot my birthday and I really do not like this.'

You hold a flexible belief about the absence of the positive aspect

As I discussed in Chapter 2, holding a flexible belief in this context means that you assert your preference that a positive aspect be present, but you do not demand that it must be present. Thus, in our example, you think:

'I wish that my partner had not forgotten my birthday, but sadly and regretfully he does not have to remember it.'

You recognise that all the conditions are or were in place for the positive aspect to be absent and therefore you acknowledge that it 'should' empirically be absent

With reference to the positive aspect being absent, we can say that it 'should' empirically be absent because all the conditions were in place for it to be absent. Applying this principle to our example, you think: 'I know that my partner tends to forget important dates like my birthday and as that is the way he is, then he should have forgotten my birthday.'

You do not depreciate life for the absence of the positive aspect

Here you again acknowledge that it is not possible to evaluate life globally when you don't get what you want because life is far too complex to warrant such a global rating.

'Life is not bad for allowing my partner to forget my birthday.'

You assert the facts about life

Here, while focusing on the absence of the positive aspect you assert that life is a complex mixture of positive, negative and neutral aspects.

'While it is bad that my partner forgot my birthday, life is a complex mixture of the good, the bad and the neutral and this fact does not change even if my partner were to remember my birthday.'

This point again demonstrates the unconditional nature of unconditional life-acceptance in that life is seen to be unchanged whether the positive aspect is absent or not.

You attempt to bring into existence the positive aspect if it is possible to do so and if the benefits outweigh the costs of doing so

Again, this principle asserts that an important part of acceptance is attempting to change reality if it can be changed – in this case to bring into existence the desired, but absent positive aspect of life. I want to emphasise again that acceptance in REBT does not advocate resignation. Also, note again that change attempts are made after the implementation of the previous two anti-disturbance principles.

In our example, when initiating attempts to effect change you may, for example, speak to your partner, telling him how you feel about him forgetting your birthday, and work with him so that he remembers important dates, like your birthday, in the future.

However, as with dealing with the presence of a negative aspect, you will also weigh up the perceived benefits and costs of encouraging your partner to remember important dates. If he is the kind of person to deliberately not buy you a birthday card and present *because* you have reminded him then you may decide that it is not in your healthy interests to do so.

You hold a flexible belief about the outcome of your attempts to bring the positive aspect into existence

Here, you want a good outcome from your attempts to bring the positive aspect into existence, but you do not demand that you must be successful in this regard. In our example, you think: 'I want my partner to respond constructively to my attempts to get him to remember important dates like my birthday, but I don't have to succeed in this regard.'

*If you cannot bring the positive aspect into
existence or you recognise that it is not worth
trying to do so, you acknowledge that this is the
case, recognise that you don't like this, but also
recognise that you can move on with your life
without being preoccupied with the continuing
absence of the positive aspect*

If your attempts to bring the positive aspect into existence are
unsuccessful, acceptance means acknowledging that you don't like
this, but resolving to move on with your life without being preoccupied with the continuing absence of the positive aspect. Thus,
in our example, if having heard what you have to say your partner
continues to forget important dates such as your birthday, then
you acknowledge that you don't like this, but that you can get on
with your life despite this fact.

Unconditional self-acceptance

Unconditional self-acceptance is a belief about yourself where
certain facts about you are asserted and certain fictions about you
are negated. In what follows, I will exemplify my points by referring to a situation where you dislike the presence of a negative
aspect of yourself which, in this example, is a large nose. The same
steps and points apply to accepting yourself for the absence of a
positive aspect.

*You acknowledge both the presence of the
negative aspect and the fact that you don't like
its presence*

'I have a large nose and I don't like it.'

*You hold a flexible belief about the presence of
the negative aspect*

'I wish that I had a smaller nose, but it is not necessary that I
have one.'

You recognise that all the conditions are in place for the negative aspect to be present and therefore you acknowledge that it 'should' empirically be present

> 'I have the nose that I have. It is probably a genetic heritage from my parents. Therefore, I should have the nose that I have. That is the reality that I am facing.'

You do not depreciate yourself for having the negative aspect

Here, you acknowledge that it is not possible to evaluate yourself globally when you don't have what you want because you are far too complex as a human being to warrant such a global rating.

> 'I am not a defective person for having a large nose.'

You assert the facts about yourself

Here, you assert that you are a unique, unrateable, complex, fallible human being when focusing on the negative aspect.

> 'I am a fallible human being with many aspects, positive, negative and neutral, and this fact does not change about me just because I have a large nose.'

This point demonstrates the unconditional nature of unconditional self-acceptance in that your 'self' is seen to be unchanged whether the negative aspect is present or not (in our example, whether you have a large nose or not).

You attempt to change the negative aspect if it can be changed and if the benefits outweigh the costs of doing so

If you depreciate yourself for having a negative aspect (such as a large nose) you may well try to change it even though the long-term costs may outweigh the benefits. Thus, you may decide to have an operation on your nose when it is not really indicated and when doing so will put you into a good deal of debt. However, if you think about doing so from the vantage point of self-acceptance then you may decide not to have the operation under the same circumstances.

You hold a flexible belief about the outcome of your attempts to change the negative aspect

If you do attempt to change the negative aspect, then it is best to do so when you hold a flexible belief about the outcome of your change attempts. Thus, if you do decide to have an operation on your nose, the healthiest way of doing so is to think that while you want it to work out in the desired manner, sadly and regretfully it does not have to do so and, indeed, you may end up by making matters worse rather than better. This flexible belief will prepare you to deal healthily with a less than desired outcome of your attempts to change the negative aspect.

If you cannot change the negative aspect or you recognise that it is not worth doing so, you acknowledge that this is the case, recognise that you don't like this, but also recognise that you can move on with your life without being preoccupied with the continuing presence of the negative aspect

I want to reiterate here what I said in the section on unconditional life-acceptance. If your attempts to change the negative aspect are unsuccessful or if the costs of trying to do so outweigh the benefits, acceptance means acknowledging that you don't like this, but resolving to move on with your life without being preoccupied with the continuing presence of the negative aspect. Thus, in our example, if you decide that changing the size of your nose is too expensive for you, then you acknowledge that while you don't like the fact that you will have to continue to live with your large nose, you can get on with your life despite this fact.

Unconditional other-acceptance

Unconditional other-acceptance is a belief about another person (or group of people) where certain facts about that person are asserted and certain fictions about him (in this case) are negated. In what follows, I will exemplify my points by referring to a situation where you again dislike the presence of a negative aspect of another person, which, in this example, is excessive noise from a neighbour. The same steps and points apply to accepting another person for the absence of a positive aspect.

You acknowledge both the presence of the negative aspect and the fact that you don't like its presence

'I don't like the fact that my neighbour makes a lot of noise.'

You hold a flexible belief about the presence of the negative aspect

'I wish that my neighbour was not noisy, but it does not follow that he must be the way I want him to be.'

You recognise that all the conditions are in place for the negative aspect to be present and therefore you acknowledge that it 'should' empirically be present

'The reality is that my neighbour is noisy. Why is he like that? Probably because of a number of factors that I don't know about which obviously lead him to behave in a noisy manner. Therefore, my neighbour empirically has to be noisy as long as he is that way.'

You do not depreciate the other person for having the negative aspect

Here you acknowledge that it is not possible to evaluate your neighbour globally when he acts in a way that you don't like because he is far too complex as a human being to warrant such a global rating.

'My neighbour is not a bad person for being noisy.'

You assert the facts about the other person

Here, you assert that your neighbour is a unique, unrateable, complex, fallible human being when focusing on the negative aspect.

> 'My neighbour is a fallible human being with many aspects, positive, negative and neutral and this fact does not change about him just because he is noisy.'

This point demonstrates the unconditional nature of unconditional other-acceptance in that the other person is seen to be unchanged whether the negative aspect is present or not (in our example, whether your neighbour is noisy or not).

You attempt to change the negative aspect if it can be changed and if the benefits outweigh the costs of doing so

If you depreciate your neighbour for having a negative aspect (i.e. being noisy) you may well try to change this even though the long-term costs may outweigh the benefits. Thus, you may decide to assert yourself with your neighbour even though you know, for example, that he has a violent temper. However, if you think about doing so from the vantage point of other-acceptance then you may decide not to assert yourself under the same circumstances.

You hold a flexible belief about the outcome of your attempts to change the negative aspect

If you do attempt to change the negative aspect, then it is best to do so when you hold a flexible belief about the outcome of your change attempts. Thus, if you do decide to assert yourself with your neighbour, the healthiest way of doing so is to think that while you want your neighbour to stop being noisy as a result of talking to him, sadly he does not have to do so and you may end up by making matters worse rather than better. This flexible belief will prepare you to deal healthily with a less than desired outcome of your attempts to change the negative aspect.

If you cannot change the negative aspect or you recognise that it is not worth doing so, you acknowledge that this is the case, recognise that you don't like this, but also recognise that you can move on with your life without being preoccupied with the continuing presence of the negative aspect

I want to reiterate here what I said in the sections on unconditional life-acceptance and unconditional self-acceptance. If your attempts to change the negative aspect are unsuccessful or if the costs of trying to do so outweigh the benefits, acceptance means acknowledging that you don't like this, but resolving to move on with your life without being preoccupied with the continuing presence of the negative aspect. Thus, in our example, if you have tried to persuade your neighbour to stop being noisy and you failed to do so, or if you have decided that trying to persuade your neighbour is counterproductive, then you acknowledge that while you don't like the fact that you will have to continue to live with a noisy neighbour, you can get on with your life despite this fact.

Determining whether a belief is an acceptance belief or a depreciation belief

As I have mentioned in the previous three chapters, when attempting to ascertain whether a person holds a rational belief (in this case, a non-extreme acceptance belief) or an irrational belief (in this case, an extreme depreciation belief), it is important to examine the consequences of such beliefs.

Thus, if the person holds a non-extreme acceptance belief, he will tend to experience the following consequences:

• Healthy negative emotions
• Constructive behaviours and action tendencies
• Realistic and balanced subsequent thinking.

And if the person holds an extreme depreciation belief, he will tend to experience:

• Unhealthy negative emotions
• Unconstructive behaviours and action tendencies

- Highly distorted subsequent thinking that is heavily skewed to the negative.

Let me illustrate this by revisiting the cases of Cynthia and Linda whom we met in the previous three chapters. If you recall, they were made redundant from their jobs in the same company on the same day. Their jobs were equally important to them and therefore the loss of their job was equivalent in meaning to both.

Cynthia was depressed about the loss because she believed that it proved that she was a loser. This led her to experience the same consequences as she did when holding a rigid belief, an awfulising belief and a discomfort intolerance belief about the job loss. Thus, she withdrew into herself and did not make any attempt to apply for new jobs. Rather than seek and use support from her family and friends, she claimed things were hopeless and accused people of not being sympathetic whenever they made helpful suggestions. She had the following thoughts: 'Because I am a loser, this means that I will always lose, so it's not worth trying to get another job' and 'As a loser, I will lose out not only at work but in all other areas of my life as well'. These subsequent thoughts are, as can be seen, highly distorted and very skewed to the negative.

Linda, on the other hand, was sad, but not depressed about being made redundant because she believed that while it was bad to lose her job, she was not a loser, but a fallible human being whose worth as a person is dependent upon being alive and not on having a job. As with her flexible, non-awfulising and discomfort tolerance beliefs, this self-acceptance belief led her to acknowledge and work through her loss, to stay connected with others, to apply for new jobs, and to seek and use support from friends and family members. Needless to say, Linda found a new job quite quickly, whereas Cynthia remained unemployed for much longer. Linda had the following thoughts: 'Getting a job may be difficult, but if I keep trying, I will probably get one' and 'Even if I don't get a job, I will recover from the loss and can still find meaning and pleasure in life'. These thoughts are realistic and balanced rather than highly distorted and heavily skewed to the negative.

Why acceptance beliefs are rational or healthy

We have seen that in REBT, beliefs are rational or healthy if they meet three criteria:

- They are true.
- They are logical.
- They have healthy consequences.

By these criteria, acceptance beliefs are rational or healthy. Let me elaborate.

Unconditional acceptance beliefs are true

An unconditional acceptance belief points to your attitude towards yourself, others and life and acknowledges certain facts about the objects of your acceptance. I will distinguish here between unconditional person-acceptance beliefs and unconditional life-acceptance beliefs. I will begin by considering unconditional person-acceptance.

Unconditional person-acceptance beliefs are true

If you hold an unconditional person-acceptance belief you acknowledge that a person (yourself and others) is:

- human
- too complex to be rated legitimately as a whole although aspects of him or her can be rated
- unique
- fallible
- in flux
- capable of change.

Unconditional person-acceptance beliefs are true, therefore, in that all the above attributes are accurate descriptions of the nature of a person and they hold true no matter what the person does or what happens to him (this latter point is the unconditional component of an unconditional person-acceptance belief).

Unconditional life-acceptance beliefs are true

If you hold an unconditional life-acceptance belief you acknowledge that life is:

- too complex to be rated legitimately as a whole although aspects of life can be rated
- comprised of positive, negative and neutral aspects
- in flux
- capable of being changed.

Unconditional life-acceptance beliefs are true, therefore, in that all the above attributes are accurate descriptions of the nature of life and they hold true no matter what happens in life (this latter point is the unconditional component of an unconditional life-acceptance belief).

A component analysis and the truth of unconditional acceptance beliefs

Let's look at the proposition that acceptance beliefs are true in a different way. An acceptance belief has three components which I will illustrate by considering an unconditional self-acceptance belief, but which also applies to an unconditional other-acceptance belief and an unconditional life-acceptance belief.

An unconditional self-acceptance belief has three components:

1   The 'aspect evaluation' component. Here you evaluate negatively an aspect of yourself or what happens to you (e.g. 'It is bad that I have a large nose').
2   The 'negated depreciation' component, where you negate the idea that you can be rated negatively as a whole for the negative aspect (e.g. 'I am not defective for having a large nose').
3   The 'asserted acceptance' component, where you assert the facts about yourself. (e.g. 'Rather I am a unique, fallible human being with a larger nose than I would like'). All these components are true as we shall see below.

The 'aspect evaluation' component is true

First, you can prove that having a large nose has negative aspects. For example, it goes against your desire for a smaller nose, many people (but far from all) will dislike it and think you look less attractive than you would do if your nose were smaller, and it may hamper you in certain careers (e.g. the media). We may also say, parenthetically, that having a large nose may have positive aspects, but let's assume that the bad aspects overshadow the good and let's assume further, therefore, that it is true to say:

'It is bad to have a large nose.'

The 'negated depreciation' component is true

Second, you can prove that you are not defective for having a large nose. If you were defective then you would have to be scrapped because you would have no use and no one would want to know you. So we can truthfully say:

'I am not defective for having a large nose.'

The 'asserted acceptance' component is true

Third, you can prove that the following defining aspects of you are true:

'I am a unique, fallible, unrateable, human being who has a large nose and these defining features of me will not change even if I have the nose that I want.'

So, in summary, when you consider the three components of your unconditional self-acceptance belief, you can see that all parts are true and therefore the unconditional self-acceptance belief is true.

(1) 'It is bad to have a large nose . . . (2) . . . but I am not defective for having one . . . (3) Rather I am a fallible, unrateable, human being who has a large nose and these defining features of me will not change even if I have the nose that I want.'

I summarise all these points in Table 6.

Table 6 Unconditional self-acceptance and self-depreciation beliefs, their components and their emotional consequences

Self-depreciation belief	Aspect evaluation component	Depreciation component		Emotion
'I am defective for having a large nose'	'It is bad that I have a large nose . . .	. . . and therefore I am defective'		Depression

Unconditional self-acceptance belief	Aspect evaluation component	Negated depreciation component	Asserted acceptance component	Emotion
'It is bad that I have a large nose, but I am not defective. Rather I am a fallible, unrateable, human being who has a large nose and these defining features will not change even if I have the nose that I want'	'It is bad that I have a large nose . . .	. . . but I am not defective . . .	. . . Rather I am a fallible, unrateable, human being who has a large nose and these defining features will not change even if I have the nose that I want'	Disappointment

Unconditional acceptance beliefs are logical

In this section, I will consider unconditional self-acceptance beliefs, but the same points also apply to unconditional other-acceptance and unconditional life-acceptance beliefs.

When considering whether or not an unconditional self-acceptance belief is logical, we need to consider what philosophers call the part-whole error. This error describes a situation where you define the whole of something on the basis of one of its parts. In our example, when you hold an unconditional self-acceptance belief, you are *not* making the part-whole error. Rather, you are highlighting your complexity as a human being which incorporates, but is not changed by, the negative aspect under focus.

Thus, when we take the three components of an unconditional self-acceptance belief (as outlined above), the following two points make clear that an unconditional self-acceptance belief is logical:

- The part-whole error is explicitly negated.
  'It is bad to have a large nose' [part] $\longrightarrow$ 'I am not defective for having a large nose' [whole]
- The whole incorporates the part.
  'It is bad to have a large nose' [part] $\longrightarrow$ 'Rather I am a fallible, unrateable, human being who has a large nose and these defining aspects of me will not change even if I have the nose that I want' [whole]

Unconditional acceptance beliefs are helpful

First, unconditional acceptance beliefs tend to lead to one or more of the following healthy negative emotions when you encounter adversities: concern, sadness, remorse, disappointment, sorrow, healthy anger, healthy jealousy and healthy envy. Second, unconditional acceptance beliefs tend to lead to constructive behaviour in the face of negative activating events such as: facing up to and dealing with difficult situations, sensible working hours, healthy exercise patterns and healthy eating and drinking patterns. Third, unconditional acceptance beliefs tend to lead to subsequent realistic thinking, such as making realistic estimates of adversities happening, viewing positive events as equally as likely to occur as negative events, seeing negative events in perspective and in a sensible context, and making an objective appraisal of your coping resources.

Holding unconditional acceptance beliefs leads to similar consequences to those that stem from flexibility, non-awfulising beliefs and discomfort tolerance beliefs

As we have just seen, when you hold an unconditional acceptance belief when facing an adversity, you will experience a number of emotional, behavioural and cognitive effects that will increase your chances of changing the adversity if it can be changed or of adjusting constructively to it if it cannot be changed. However, there are other positive aspects of holding unconditional acceptance beliefs and because these beliefs stem from flexibility these positive aspects are the same as those I discussed in Chapter 2 (see pp. 19–26). I will once again summarise these consequences here, but suggest that you refer to pp. 19–26 for an extended discussion of this issue.

Unconditional acceptance beliefs help you to:

- 'roll with the punches' when hit by an adversity
- adjust to change
- initiate constructive change
- embrace complexity
- be creative.

Working towards holding unconditional acceptance beliefs as a goal

As I pointed out in Chapter 2, rationality is a state towards which we strive rather than a state that can be achieved once and for all. In the same way as we can work towards being more flexible (see Chapter 2), towards holding non-awfulising beliefs in the face of adversity (see Chapter 3) and towards tolerating adversity (Chapter 4), we can also work towards holding unconditional acceptance beliefs under such circumstances. If we can work towards increasing the times when we hold non-extreme, unconditional acceptance beliefs and decreasing the times when we hold extreme, depreciation beliefs, then we are working towards psychological health.

Thus, if in a specific situation, you begin by holding a depreciation belief, this is not necessarily a sign of psychological disturbance since it is possible for you to stand back and change this belief to its non-extreme, unconditional acceptance alternative. As will be seen from the next section, engaging in a struggle between holding a depreciation belief and an unconditional acceptance belief is a common feature of psychological health as long as you end up by holding the unconditional acceptance belief.

Three realistic unconditional acceptance credos

In this final section, I will outline three realistic unconditional acceptance credos. The first will focus on unconditional self-acceptance (USA), the second on unconditional other-acceptance (UOA) and the third on unconditional life-acceptance (ULA). I will put these credos in the first person and as you read them bear in mind that they are general credos which need to be applied to specific situations.

A realistic unconditional self-acceptance credo

As a human being I recognise that when adversities occur and I think that I have been the author of them, I may tend to depreciate myself, particularly when I demand that I absolutely should have done what I did not do or that I absolutely should not have done what I did. It is a real struggle for me to accept myself in such circumstances, particularly when my contribution to the adversities has been great, but I can do so. In the journey towards unconditional self-acceptance, I may well do many things to deal with my disturbed feelings which may help me in the short term, but not in the long term. Thus, I may deny that I feel disturbed and say either that I am not bothered about what happened or that I am handling it well. I may also deny responsibility for bringing about the adversity, preferring to blame others or life conditions. However, I recognise that denial is not healthy and will use this as a cue to think rationally about myself as soon as I am able. While I recognise that I can do this, I also acknowledge that there will be times when I won't. The path towards holding unconditional self-acceptance beliefs is a rocky one. When I do eventually think in this non-extreme, self-accepting way, I will accept that when adversities happen and I am responsible for them, I will feel badly about my behaviour, but not about myself. Rather, I will see that I am a unique, fallible, unrateable, complex, ever-changing individual and can choose to accept myself as such even though I will continue to dislike my bad behaviour. However, I also recognise that it is very difficult for me to hold self-acceptance beliefs when I am responsible for adversities and to keep these beliefs non-extreme. As such, I will return to disturbed negative feelings when I go back to holding extreme self-depreciation beliefs.

While self-acceptance beliefs will help me to move towards greater psychological health, I recognise that even when I work hard to develop such beliefs, I will often return to thinking in a self-depreciating manner. Similarly, I acknowledge that as I work to internalise this realistic credo, I will experience many lapses along the way. The best way of dealing with these lapses is to accept them, without liking them, learn specific things from them and act on such specific learning in relevant future situations.

When I acknowledge that holding self-acceptance beliefs is healthy this becomes another positive in my life. As such, I may depreciate myself if I do not think in this non-extreme way, which paradoxically is evidence that I am in fact thinking in an extreme self-depreciating manner. When this happens, I will recognise that I am depreciating myself about holding a self-depreciating belief and will work towards thinking in a more self-accepting way about my self-depreciating beliefs. I will do this by showing myself that while it is bad to depreciate myself, doing so does not define me, and that I am a fallible human being who may well lapse into self-depreciation even though I know it is irrational to do so. Doing this will help me get back on the path towards greater self-acceptance.

A realistic unconditional other-acceptance credo

As a human being I recognise that when adversities occur and I think that another person is responsible for them, I may tend to depreciate that person, particularly when I demand that he (in this case) absolutely should have done what he did not do or that he absolutely should not have done what he did. It is a real struggle for me to accept that person in such circumstances, particularly when his contribution to the adversities has been great, but I can do so. In the journey towards unconditional other-acceptance, I recognise that I may well do many things to deal with my disturbed feelings which may help me in the short term, but not in the long term. Thus, I may express my disturbed feelings in ways that feel good in the moment and I may also say either that I am not bothered about what happened or that I am handling it well. However, I recognise that catharsis and denial are not healthy responses in the longer term and will use these as cues to think rationally about the other person as soon as I am able. While I recognise that I can do this, I also acknowledge that there will be times when I won't. The path towards holding uncon-ditional other-acceptance beliefs is a rocky one. When I do eventually think in this non-extreme, other-accepting way, I will accept that when adversities happen and another person is responsible for them,

I will feel badly about that person's behaviour, but will not condemn him as a person. Rather, I will see that he is a unique, fallible, unrateable, complex, ever-changing individual and that I can choose to accept him as such even though I will continue to dislike his behaviour. However, I also recognise that it is very difficult for me to hold other-acceptance beliefs when the other person is responsible for adversities and to keep these beliefs non-extreme. As such, I will return to disturbed negative feelings when I go back to holding extreme other-depreciation beliefs.

While other-acceptance beliefs will help me to move towards greater psychological health, I recognise that even when I work hard to develop such beliefs, I will often return to thinking in an other-depreciating manner. Similarly, I acknowledge that as I work to internalise this realistic credo, I will experience many lapses along the way. The best way of dealing with these lapses is to accept them, without liking them, learn specific things from them and act on such specific learning in relevant future situations.

When I acknowledge that holding other-acceptance beliefs is healthy this becomes another positive in my life. As such, I may depreciate myself if I do not think in this non-extreme way. When this happens, I will recognise that I am depreciating myself about holding an other-depreciating belief and will work towards thinking in a more self-accepting way about my other-depreciating beliefs. I will do this by showing myself that while it is bad to depreciate another person, doing so does not define me, and that I am a fallible human being who may well lapse into other-depreciation even though I know it is irrational to do so. Doing this will help me get back on the path towards greater other-acceptance.

A realistic unconditional life-acceptance credo

As a human being I recognise that when adversities occur and I think that life conditions are responsible for them, I may tend to depreciate life, particularly when I demand that life absolutely should be the way I want it to be or absolutely should not be the way I don't want it to be. It is a real struggle for me to accept life in such circumstances, particularly when its contribution to the adversities has been great, but I can do so. In the journey towards unconditional life-acceptance, I recognise that I may well do many things to deal with my disturbed feelings which may help me in the short term, but not in the long term. Thus, I may express my disturbed feelings in ways that feel good in the moment and I may also say either that I am not bothered about what happened or that I am handling it well. However, I recognise that catharsis and denial are not healthy responses in the longer term and will use these as cues to think rationally about life as soon as I am able. While I recognise that I can do this, I also acknowledge that there will be times when I won't. The path towards holding unconditional life-acceptance beliefs is a rocky one. When I do eventually think in this non-extreme, life-accepting way, I will accept that when adversities happen and life conditions are responsible for them, I will feel badly about that aspect of life, but will not depreciate life in its entirety. Rather, I will see that life is a complicated mixture of the good, the bad and the neutral and that I can choose to accept life as such even though I will continue to dislike that aspect of life that brought about the adversity. However, I also recognise that it is very difficult for me to hold life-acceptance beliefs when life is responsible for adversities and to keep these beliefs non-extreme. As such, I will return to disturbed negative feelings when I go back to holding extreme life-depreciation beliefs.

While life-acceptance beliefs will help me to move towards greater psychological health, I recognise that even when I work hard to develop such beliefs, I will often return to thinking in a life-depreciating manner. Similarly, I acknowledge that as I work to internalise this realistic credo, I will experience many lapses along the way. The best way of dealing with these lapses is to accept them, without liking them, learn specific things from them and act on such specific learning in relevant future situations.

When I acknowledge that holding life-acceptance beliefs is healthy this becomes another positive in my life. As such, I may depreciate myself if I do not think in this non-extreme way. When this happens, I will recognise that I am depreciating myself about holding a life-depreciating belief and will work towards thinking in a more self-accepting way about my life-depreciating beliefs. I will do this by showing myself that while it is bad to depreciate life, doing so does not define me, and that I am a fallible human being who may well lapse into life-depreciation even though I know it is irrational to do so. Doing this will help me get back on the path towards greater life-acceptance.

So what are the advantages and disadvantages of realistic unconditional acceptance credos? They are similar to those of the realistic flexibility, non-awfulising and discomfort tolerance credos that I discussed in Chapters 2, 3 and 4. The advantages seem to be as follows:

1   It gives people a warts-and-all picture of acceptance that is within the grasp of most people.
2   Even though periods of depreciation and denial are present in realistic acceptance, there is still a clear indication of the rational thinking that people should aim for.
3   It can comfort rather than inspire and can thus motivate those people who value realism in their quest for greater acceptance.

However, there are disadvantages to the realistic unconditional acceptance credos, as there are with the realistic flexibility credo, the realistic non-awfulising credo and the discomfort tolerance credo:

1   They may legitimise disturbance and denial as necessary components of acceptance, whereas, in reality, they are frequently rather than inevitably occurring components.
2   They may discourage those people who are capable of a more ideal form of acceptance (i.e. one relatively free from disturbance and denial) from seeing acceptance as a legitimate goal.

However, in my view the advantages of these realistic acceptance credos outweigh their disadvantages and, given their realistic nature, it is useful for a person to apply them when striving to hold self-acceptance, other-acceptance and life-acceptance beliefs in the face of adversities.

I have now considered the four cornerstones of psychological health from an REBT perspective: flexibility, non-awfulising, discomfort tolerance and acceptance. In the rest of the book, I will show how these beliefs can be broadly applied, beginning with the concept of self-motivation which I consider in the following chapter.

Part 2

Psychological health:
beyond the basics

Chapter 6

Self-motivation

Introduction

In this chapter, I will consider the issue of motivation and, in doing so, I will focus exclusively on self-motivation and will not discuss the concept of motivating others. In particular, and in keeping with the theme of this book, I will highlight the healthy aspects of self-motivation, although I will also discuss times when motivation may not lead to such healthy results for the individual.

The concept of motivation is somewhat elusive. It can refer to a sense of enthusiasm for doing something or to a reason for doing that same thing. It can relate to the impact of higher psychological factors or of more basic biologically-based factors on behaviour. It can also point to factors that influence behaviour that are within the person's conscious awareness, as well as to those factors that are outside the person's conscious awareness. Finally, it can refer to factors within the person that drive behaviour, as well as to external factors such as rewards or penalties that can either encourage or discourage behaviour.

In considering self-motivation, I will cover the following:

1   Self-motivation and reasons
2   Self-motivation and feelings
3   Self-motivation and the hierarchy of needs

Self-motivation and reasons

One of the main factors that explains why we motivate ourselves to do something is that we have a reason to do so. A reason (some-times confusingly known as a motive) is fundamentally a cognition, although, like almost all cognitions, it often involves an emotion and a tendency to act in a certain way.

Reasons and goals

Quite often the reason that we act in a certain way is that we think that this action will help us to achieve a goal or an outcome. Such goals may be the presence of something that we want (I call these 'positive goals') or the absence of something that we don't want (I call these 'negative goals').

Positive and negative goals

When a person has a positive goal, then her motivation to achieve this goal is likely to be stronger than it is to achieve a negative goal, assuming that all other things are equal. The reason for this is that it is easier to work towards something when you can clearly see what it is you are aiming for, which is the case with a positive goal.

The trouble with a negative goal (which I have defined as the achievement of an absence of something undesired) is that it is much harder to envisage. One of the reasons that practitioners of cognitive behaviour therapy (CBT), on which this book is based, encourage their clients to convert their negative goals to positive goals is precisely to help them increase their motivation to achieve them.

Whose goals are they anyway?

People can have goals for different reasons. When a person's goal is her own, she has decided to pursue the goal because its achievement benefits her in ways that she considers to be in her own best interests. For example, Esther's goal is to get a degree in veterinary science because she wants to do research to improve the well-being of dogs.

However, a person can set a goal that has been introjected and is not her own. In this context, the word 'introjected' means swallowed whole without being digested. Now, an introjected goal may also coincide with what the person wants, but it often doesn't, and when this is the case, the person is actually pursuing a goal that she does not truly desire. For example, Sarah, a student colleague of Esther (see above), is also pursuing a degree in veterinary science.

However, she is doing so to please her father who wants her to join his veterinary practice. In reality, however, Sarah wants to be an interior designer, but she has not dared to admit this to her father. Consequently, she is studying a subject in which she has no interest, biding her time before plucking up courage to admit to her father her true vocational goal.

It is perhaps a truism to say that a person is more likely to pursue a goal that has been set by herself than one that is not her own but that has been introjected. Esther (whose goal to study veterinary science was her own) worked hard at her studies even though she found them difficult because she really wanted to get her degree. On the other hand, Sarah (whose goal to study veterinary science was not her own) found every reason not to study even though she was much brighter than Esther and found the subject easier. In common parlance, we can say that Esther was more motivated to get her degree than Sarah was to get hers.

Goals: outcomes vs. process

Goals usually refer to something a person desires that she does not currently have. For this reason they are often called 'outcome goals' since they point to an outcome of certain activities designed to achieve the person's goal. For example, if your outcome goal is to have completed an essay, then you have an outcome in mind and you need to engage in a number of activities (e.g. reading material, structuring the essay based on your reading, drafting the essay and then writing the final draft) which are designed to help you to achieve your goal.

Process: enjoyable or not?

I regard activities in which you engage in the service of achieving an outcome goal as process factors. Now, it makes a difference if you enjoy engaging in these process activities, in that you are more likely to engage in tasks that you enjoy than in tasks that you don't enjoy. Such enjoyment may be motivating in itself since you will seek out such enjoyment for its own sake as well as because engaging in these activities will help you to achieve your outcome goal. I will discuss this further presently.

If you don't enjoy engaging in these process activities then you need to focus your attention on the reasons why you want to achieve your outcome goals rather than on your lack of enjoyment of the instrumental activities. In doing so, you need to hold the belief that while it would be better if you did enjoy these process tasks, you don't have to enjoy them in order to do them. In essence, you will be doing undesired tasks in order to achieve your desired goal.

On the other hand, if you do enjoy these process tasks then you have two forms of motivation: (1) the motivation to do the tasks because they lead to you achieving your desired outcome goal, and (2) the motivation to do the tasks because you enjoy doing them. Needless to say, people who have both types of motivation are more likely to do the relevant tasks and to achieve their goals than people who are motivated in only one of these two ways.

Reasons, goals and time-frames

On page 90, we met Esther who wanted to get a veterinary degree because she wanted to do research into helping sick dogs. However, Esther was also very sociable and liked to go out with her university friends, but she did not allow her short-term enjoyment to take precedence over her longer-term goals. By careful self-management and work planning she managed to stay on track with her work and participate in some, but not all, of the social activities which attracted her.

Esther's example shows that a person can have short-term and long-term motivation to pursue different things and that one can give priority to one's long-term goals and yet, through careful planning, get some of one's short-term desires met.

We also met Sarah on pp. 90–91. If you recall, Sarah was more intellectually able than Esther, but did not want to pursue a career in veterinary science. She was interested in having a good time. She had short-term motivation to be at college (to have a good time), but did not have long-term motivation to be there. She thus did very little work (just enough to stay at college to pursue her hedonistic lifestyle), but took every opportunity to engage in social activities that interested her, which was most of them.

Belinda was another student on the same degree course as Esther and Sarah. She was as motivated as Esther to get her veterinary science degree, but did not temper this by pursuing any short-term goals. Consequently, she spent all the time working for her degree without taking any breaks to engage in other non-work-related pursuits. Being so blinkered had a very negative consequence for Belinda as, after a while, she experienced burn-out, and by the time her first-year exams came around, she was so exhausted she could not sit them.

Finally we have Fiona who was also a student on the same course. Like Sarah, Fiona went to university to study for a veterinary science degree to please her parents. Thus, like Sarah, she lacked a long-term motivation to study. However, unlike Sarah, she had no interest in participating in any of the many social activities that were going on at university. Thus, as well as lacking a long-term motivation for being at university. Fiona lacked a short-term motivation for being there. As a result, Fiona spent her days either in her room in bed or aimlessly walking around the campus having numerous cups of coffee and smoking endless cigarettes. Needless to say, after a while, Fiona became depressed.

Out of the four cases that I have outlined and discussed, the case of Esther illustrates the healthiest way forward in terms of motivation. While at first sight it may appear that being devoted to a long-term goal to the exclusion of anything else might help a person to achieve that goal, as the case of Belinda shows, after a while a person may experience burn-out and not have the energy to keep going over the long haul. Extrapolating from the maxim 'All work and no play makes Jack a dull boy', we see from this vignette that: 'All work and no play makes Belinda an exhausted girl.'

By contrast, as Esther showed, achieving a balance between pursuing one's long-term goals and pursuing one's short-term goals helps to sustain the person as she works towards achieving her long-term goals. To quote another aphorism, 'Having a little of what you enjoy does you good!'

Real reasons vs. expressed, but false reasons

What motivates a person may be very different from what he says motivates him. According to psychologists, people have a tendency to present themselves in a favourable light to other people, in order to seek approval or to ward off disapproval. Here is an example of this discrepancy. Malcolm established a foundation to teach deaf students how to play a musical instrument and raised a lot of money for this organisation. His real reason for doing so was to receive an honour from the Queen, but he did not admit to this. When pressed, he would say that his motivation was purely to help students get joy from playing music. After ten years, Malcolm lost interest and closed his foundation when he failed to receive his hoped-for honour and learned on the grapevine that he was unlikely to receive one in the future. There is another aphorism that nicely sums up the point I am trying to make here. It is: 'Judge a man not by his words, but by his actions.'

Mixed motivations

In presenting the case of Malcolm above, I have described a situation in which he had pure and selfish motivations. His reason for establishing his foundation was only to be publicly honoured for his efforts. He had no genuine interest in helping deaf students to learn to play a musical instrument. His prior research showed that no such foundation existed and he thought that the efforts he put into his innovative foundation would get him what he wanted.

In reality, our motivations may be mixed, meaning that they may be a combination of selfless and self-interested reasons. For example, if Malcolm had been interested in the musical education of deaf students and had set up his foundation to further this end, as well as doing so to get honoured for his efforts, then we would say that he had mixed motivations.

I have a small practice and help people with their emotional problems because I genuinely would like to see people live mentally healthier lives. However, I do so now only in return for being well paid for my efforts.

However, I would not want to do work that I was not interested in even for the same amount of money. Thus, my motives are mixed rather than purely altruistic or purely financial.

Doing things for self vs. doing things for others

When I was discussing the cases of Sarah and Fiona, I made the point that both of them went to university to study veterinary science not because they wanted to do this, but because their respective parents wanted them to do so. However, doing things for others as a reason for doing something is far from always a poor motivation to do it. It was a poor motivation for Sarah and Fiona precisely because they did not want to do the degree course for themselves. However, a person can want to do something for others precisely for altruistic reasons. In this case doing things for others is a strong motivation for the person because it resonates with one of the person's values, a point I will consider presently.

Conscious and unconscious motivation

The reasons why we do things may be conscious or unconscious. While Freud did not discover the unconscious (see Ellenberger, 1970), he did bring this concept to public awareness and unconscious motivation is an important concept in psychoanalysis in explaining why we do what we do. When our motivation is conscious we know why we do what we do, although we may disguise these reasons from others (see the example of Malcolm on pp. 93–94). However, when our motivation is unconscious we may think we know the reasons for our actions, but we are likely to be wrong. This is because our behaviour has been motivated by impulses, memories and desires that we have repressed and which are thus not accessible to our conscious mind.

Our motivation may be pre-conscious rather than unconscious. When this is the case, the reasons why we act in the way we do are not immediately apparent to us, but we can fairly easily be helped or help ourselves to discern this motivation. By contrast, understanding motivation that is unconscious is far harder, more time-consuming and usually involves the help of a suitably trained professional.

The motivational power of reasons based on values and principles

Perhaps the most profound form of motivation involves reasons that are based on a person's values and principles. Before we proceed with this discussion let me distinguish between a value and a principle. A value is an established ideal of life, while a principle is a fundamental belief, a rule of action or conduct, a truth that is a foundation for other truths. In this case a principle may be said to be more basic than a value and, in fact, to underpin it.

A person may verbally claim to hold a particular value or principle, but whether the person's behaviour is actually motivated by that particular value or principle is another matter, as one can espouse a particular value or principle and not be motivated by it, a point that I will discuss later in this section.

However, when a person's behaviour is actually motivated by a value or by a principle, particularly one that is held very dear, then it can take a lot for that person not to act in ways that are consistent with that value or principle. This is why soldiers at the outbreak of war are exhorted to remember that they are going to war not just to defend their country but also to defend core principles such as freedom and democracy. Thus, if they were to die in the ensuing battle their death would not be in vain but in the service of both their country and the particular values that were being defended.

Speaking of death, the case of Thomas à Becket illustrates powerfully the profound impact that a central principle has as a motivator on a person's behaviour. Thomas à Becket was Archbishop of Canterbury when Henry VIII was on the throne of England. Henry wanted Becket as Archbishop to approve the Constitutions of Clarendon which asserted the King's right to 'punish criminous clerks, forbade excommunication of royal officials and appeals to Rome and gave the King the revenues of vacant sees and the power to influence Episcopal elections' (Encyclopaedia Britannica online: Saint Thomas Becket). Thomas à Becket claimed that these constitutions contravened church law and refused to approve them even though he knew that he might pay for it with his life, which indeed is what happened.

I am not suggesting that people should die rather than act in ways that are inconsistent with their core values or principles. Rather, my aim is to show the power of value-based and principle-based reasons as motivators of behaviour. Indeed, preserving one's life is often a central principle for people, although some people are prepared to die to save the life of a loved one. For this latter group of people preserving the life of a loved one is a higher-order principle than saving one's own life.

When a person contemplates acting in ways that are inconsistent with cherished values or principles he may say things like 'I couldn't live with myself if I did that', indicating a view that Thomas à Becket put into practice. For most of the rest of us, however, if we do find ourselves acting against our values or principles we search for reasons for doing so that permit us to live with ourselves, albeit uncomfortably. I say all of this to underscore the point once again that value-based and principle-based reasons are powerful forms of motivation and will sustain a person's behaviour over the long haul.

Values and principles can clash

People do not just have one or two values or principles to motivate them. They have a complex network of values and principles, some of which might clash with others. When this occurs, a person may be said to experience a value-based or principle-based conflict which may impair action.

Why people do not act on their values or principles

I made the point earlier that people may not act according to their values or principles. This may happen for a number of reasons.

1   The person may not have their value or principle in mind when acting in a certain way.

Values and principles are general, somewhat theoretical, constructs and their relevance to behaviour in specific situations may not always be apparent to a person. However, once reminded by self or by others of the applicability of a particular value or principle to a relevant situation, the person may well then be motivated to act according to the value or principle concerned. In therapy, reminding someone of a relevant personally-held value or principle may clarify for the person how to act in a particular situation.

2   The person may be more strongly motivated to fulfil a short-term goal which is not in line with his value or principle.

One of the major themes running through this book is our struggle to reconcile our short-term and long-term goals when they conflict with one another. Thus, a common reason why a person may not be motivated to act in a way that is consistent with a relevant value or principle is because his present motivation to meet a short-term goal is stronger. When this happens, the person's attention is focused on satisfying his short-term goal and if he thinks of his conflicting relevant value or principle at all, this is likely to be at the back of his mind. However, both forms of motivation – to engage in short-term pleasure vs. to act according to one's relevant value or principle – may be at the forefront of the person's mind, and when this happens the person usually experiences an acute conflict. You may remember the Walt Disney cartoon character, Donald Duck, who would often experience such conflict. Donald would be flanked by the 'good' Donald urging him to act according to his value or principle and by the 'bad' Donald urging him to fulfil his short-term, usually unhealthy, goals. Inevitably the 'bad' would win out and I will explain why presently.

A real-life motivational conflict was experienced by Eric when he attended a conference overseas. Eric was a family man who had been happily married to his wife for fifteen years. During that time he had always been faithful to her and indeed marital fidelity was one of his core values. At the conference, Eric met a woman to whom he was physically attracted and the feelings were mutual. The woman invited Eric back to her room and after much internal turmoil between his short-term self desiring sexual satisfaction and his long-term value-based self, Eric decided to go to her room. However, after one closed-mouth kiss on the lips, Eric felt horrified at what he was about to do and made his excuses and went back to his own room. On the verge of acting against his core value, Eric brought himself back from the brink of personal disaster. Why did Eric wait till the last minute before being motivated to act according to his value of marital fidelity? When he was wrestling with his dilemma, Eric was more motivated by his short-term desire for sex than by his longer-term value. His sexual feelings were stronger than his value at that point. That is why, despite the inner turmoil, Eric went to the woman's room. However, when he kissed the woman, the acute negative feelings associated with acting against his core value became stronger than his sexual feelings. This shows the important role of feelings in motivating a person, a subject that I will discuss more fully presently.

3   The biasing effect of alcohol and drugs when one is motivated by desire-based short-term concerns and value-based long-term concerns.

As the above example shows, when a person is struggling to act in the face of different forms of motivation (desire-based short-term motivation and value-based long-term motivation) it is difficult for the person to deal productively with this struggle even when he is clear-headed. When that person is affected by drugs or alcohol, the person experiences far less of a struggle. This is due to the disinhibiting effects of such substances. When a person is in a disinhibited state, he is more likely to act in an impulsive manner than when he is not in such a state. This means that he is more likely to act to satisfy his short-term desires than his longer-term values.

If Eric had been drinking heavily before going back to his female colleague's room, then he would have experienced far less of a struggle than he actually did. Being in a disinhibited state he would have been more likely to have had sex with the woman than if he had not been drinking, and as such he would have been less likely to be mindful that in doing so he would be acting against one of his core values. However, when he had sobered up and remembered that he had had sex with his female colleague, he would then have been in turmoil because he would have been acutely aware that he had acted in a way that transgressed one of his core values.

It follows from this that it is better not to be in a disinhibited state when one is struggling in the face of desire-based short-term motivation and long-term value-based or principle-based motivation.

Rigid vs. flexible motivation

A key concept in this book, and one that I have already discussed in Chapter 2, is flexibility. In this section, I will discuss motivation that is held flexibly and contrast it to motivation that is held rigidly. I will consider the impact of rigidity and flexibility on motivation by revisiting the struggle between what I have called 'desire-based' short-term motivation and 'value-based' or 'principle-based' long-term motivation, which I first considered in the previous section.

When we are motivated by a reason to do something and this is held rigidly, we believe that we absolutely have to act in the way that is underpinned by the reason. However, when our motivation is flexible in nature we may be drawn to act in a certain way underpinned by the relevant reason, but we believe that we do not have to act in that way.

Let's revisit the case of Eric whom we first met on page 98. If you recall, Eric was tempted to sleep with a female colleague, but, after an internal struggle, decided not to do so because it conflicted with his core value of marital fidelity. If Eric had held a rigid idea about having his short-term desires met, this rigid view would have impelled him to sleep with his colleague despite the presence of his longer-term value-based motivation to be faithful to his wife. In this case, Eric's rigid belief would have had the same effect as the impact of alcohol on his decision making – he would have acted to fulfil his short-term desire at the expense of his longer-term value.

If Eric had held a rigid belief about both forms of motivation, his internal struggle would have been even more acute in the sense that he would have believed that he had to act in ways that were incompatible. In cases like this the person often turns to alcohol or drugs to relieve the tremendous internal pressure. If Eric had done this, he would have slept with the woman, for reasons that I have already discussed (see pp. 98–99).

If Eric was flexible about these different forms of motivation, he would give himself time to think clearly about his dilemma. With respect to his short-term motivation, Eric would acknowledge that he found the woman attractive and he would like to have sex with her; however, he would also hold that he did not have to act according to his short-term motivation. Also, with respect to his longer-term motivation, Eric would acknowledge that he holds marital fidelity to be a core value in his life and he would strive to act according to this value. However, he would also accept that, being human, he does not always have to live by this value. Given these two forms of flexible motivation, Eric would stand back and conduct a thorough cost-benefit analysis of whether to sleep with the woman or act according to his principle. In such a case, it is quite likely that Eric would decide to act according to his longer-term values rather than his shorter-term sexually-based feelings.

What would have happened if Eric had been flexible about his longer-term motivation and rigid about acting according to his short-term motivation. As I showed earlier, under these conditions he would have slept with the woman because his rigidity would have impelled him in this direction.

Finally, what would have happened if Eric had held a flexible view concerning his short-term motivation and a rigid view about acting according to his longer-term motivation? He would not have slept with the woman, but he might well have experienced much anxiety at the prospect that he might have done so.

So the healthiest position is where Eric holds a flexible view concerning both his 'desire-based' short-term motivation and his 'value-based' long-term motivation.

Passive reasons vs. active reasons

There is an important distinction to be made between what I call passive reasons to do something and active reasons to do something. When a reason is passive, the person can acknowledge that it is important for him to do something and can state the reason why it is important for him to do it. However, this acknowledgement does not lead the person to take appropriate action. By contrast, when a reason is active, the person not only acknowledges that it is important for him to do something and can state the reason why it is important for him to do it, he actually acts on this reason.

My view is that for a reason to be continually active, the person needs to be aware of the reason to act in a certain way, to recognise that he can choose to act on this awareness, to decide to act on this recognition and then to act on it. Thus, it is this awareness–choice–decision–action sequence that underpins active reason-based motivation.

Self-motivation and feelings

A second major form of motivation concerns our feeling states. It is a popularly held view that motivation is defined by our wish to do something. In describing this wish, we often talk about 'feeling like' doing something. Thus, when we have not done something that it is in our interests to do, we may claim that we did not do whatever it was because we did not 'feel like' doing it. This implies that 'feeling like' doing something is sufficient motivation to act in a certain way. My view is that it is not and that 'feeling-based' motivation has its problems.

However, 'feeling-based' motivation is not intrinsically problematic, particularly if the person holds a flexible view about such motivation. Let's consider the case of Gina, who is a writer, but needs to earn good money in order to live, pay her rent and have the time to devote to her writing. At the moment she waits on tables, a job that was easy to get but is poorly paid, which means that she has little time to devote to writing. Gina is a trained nurse, but does not enjoy nursing. However, if she is diligent and makes a sufficient number of job applications she should get a job as a nurse.

Gina does not 'feel like' sitting down and devoting time to making these job applications. Let's suppose that she holds a flexible view about 'feeling-based' motivation. This means that she believes that while it would be preferable if she 'felt like' doing her job applications before starting them, she recognises that this does not have to be a pre-condition for doing them. Consequently, she will do them if she reminds herself of the longer-term motivation for doing so – to get a job so that she can earn money to free herself to devote time to writing.

However, let's suppose that she holds a rigid view about 'feeling-based' motivation. This means that she believes that she has to 'feel like' doing her job applications before doing them. Consequently, she will wait until she 'feels like' doing the applications and will put off doing them until the desire to do them comes. The problem with this rigid view is that it is unproductive. The reality is that Gina does not enjoy completing application forms for jobs. If she enjoyed doing them then her rigid view of 'feeling-based' motivation would not be a problem because she would do them because she would have the desire to do them. As humans we tend to 'feel like' doing things that we enjoy and not 'feel like' doing things that we do not enjoy. The reality in Gina's case is that she finds making job applications a chore and thus she rarely, if ever, 'feels like' doing them. Consequently, given her belief that she has to 'feel like' completing application forms before she actually completes them, she invariably puts off starting them, hoping that tomorrow she may be in the mood to do them, which she rarely is. If Gina held a rigid view of 'feeling-based' motivation then she would not complete her application forms and therefore would not get a job. This would mean that she would spend all her time doing waitressing work which is poorly paid. As a result, she would not have time to devote to her writing which is what she dearly wants to do. Thus, her rigid view about 'feeling-based' motivation is clearly self-defeating.

In order to do what she wants to do, which is to devote a significant amount of her time to writing, Gina has to challenge her rigid view of 'feeling-based' motivation and develop and act on the flexible view of 'feeling-based' motivation that I discussed at the top of this page. If she did this, she would allow herself to be guided by her longer-term, 'reason-based' motivation, and she would complete and send off job applications because she had a good reason to do so.

If a person 'feels like' doing something and there is a good reason for him to do it, his 'feeling-based' motivation and reason-based motivation are working together and are a powerful motivational combination. However, when these different forms of motivation conflict, the healthy option is for the person to admit the conflict and decide which form it is in his best interests to be guided by at that particular time. This will usually be the longer-term 'reason-based' motivation. However, it is also important to recognise that when he has decided to do something for the sake of the longer-term reason, he will often get into the task and 'feel like' continuing it despite the fact that he did not 'feel like' starting it. If the person reminds himself that while he may not 'feel like' starting a task, he may well get into it after a while, then this reminder, coupled with the flexible idea that he does not have to 'feel like' doing something before starting it, will increase the chances that he will start the task and continue with it. I will develop this theme in the next chapter.

In this section, I have focused on whether or not a person 'feels like' doing something as an example of 'feeling-based' motivation. However, there are other forms of this type of motivation. Whatever form this motivation takes, the important thing is that the person holds a flexible view about it. Thus, a person may believe that it is preferable if he 'feels' determined to do something before doing it or 'feels' motivated to do it before doing it. However, since the person is flexible about these 'feelings', he is prepared to start the task in question without 'feeling' determined or without 'feeling' motivated. If the person holds a rigid view about these forms of 'feeling-based' motivation, he needs to challenge this rigid view, develop a flexible view and then repeatedly act in ways that will support and reinforce this flexible view. This means consistently beginning a task without first 'feeling' determined to do it or without first 'feeling' motivated to do it.

Maslow's hierarchy of needs and motivation

Perhaps one of the best known psychological theories is self-actualisation theory as expounded by Abraham Maslow (1968). This theory states that humans have a natural tendency to actualise themselves (i.e. develop their potential if certain conditions exist). Maslow also pointed out that humans have a variety of needs and that these can be seen as being hierarchically organised. People will tend to be motivated to meet their lower-order needs before striving to meet their higher-order needs.

In the pyramid diagram that usually depicts Maslow's hierarchy of needs, our most primitive needs are our physiological needs: breathing, food, water, sex, sleep, homeostasis and excretion. The next level up is our safety needs: security of body, of employment, of resources, of the family, of health and of property. The intermediate level concerns our needs for love and belonging and, in particular, friendship, family and sexual intimacy. Then, there are our esteem needs. These concern self-esteem, confidence, achievement, respect of others and respect by others. Finally, at the zenith of the pyramid are our self-actualisation needs which concern morality, creativity, spontaneity, problem-solving, lack of prejudice and acceptance of facts.

What Maslow argued is that one is motivated to satisfy lower-level needs before one is motivated to satisfy higher-level needs. Leaving aside the question of the definition of a need and the fact that empirical evidence has cast doubt on Maslow's theory (Wahba and Bridgewell, 1976), his scheme has pragmatic value. As stated above, the scheme argues that, for example, a man is motivated to meet his lower-level biologically-based needs, for example for food and shelter, before being motivated to meet his higher-level esteem-based or self-actualisation-based needs.

This is not universally true, however. For example, I recently went to Yad Vashem in Jerusalem (the world's premier site for the commemoration and memoralisation of the Holocaust) and saw an example of beautiful embroidery done by women in a concentration camp. What would motivate people to be creative when their freedom was severely curtailed and they were starving? The answer must be the desire of the human spirit not to be crushed even under the most dire of circumstances.

So while Maslow's point that people are motivated to meet their lower-order needs before their higher-order needs holds true generally, there are always exceptions to this rule.

A definition of healthy motivation

Based on the foregoing, I offer the following definition of healthy motivation.

> Healthy motivation occurs (i) when a person has good reasons to
> do something that he prizes, (ii) when these reasons are rooted in

important life-enhancing values and/or principles, and (iii) when he is not overly preoccupied with striving towards more basic goals. While it may be better for the person if he also (iv) 'feels like' taking the required action, the presence of such 'feeling' is secondary to the presence of value-based reasons.

A realistic rational self-motivation credo

In this final section, I will outline what I call a realistic rational self-motivation credo. This is comprised of a set of beliefs which promote realistic self-motivation. I will put this credo in the first person and as you read it bear in mind that it is a general credo which needs to be applied to specific situations.

As a human being I recognise that if I want to achieve something then I am responsible for taking action to achieve it. The ideal is for me (a) to 'feel like' taking this action, (b) to acknowledge that there is a good reason or set of reasons for me to do so, and (c) to base these reasons on values that are important to me. If these three motivational factors are present then I am very likely to take the required action to help me to achieve my goals.

It is important that I recognise that the presence of these conditions is desirable and not necessary. However, at times I may well think that one or more of these conditions are necessary and, when I do so, I will not take the required action because the needed condition or conditions are not present. However, when I realise that this is happening, I can challenge the idea that the relevant condition or conditions are necessary for me to act and can prove that this is not the case by taking the required course of action without the said condition(s) being present.

It is likely to be a real struggle for me to acknowledge that no matter how much I would like certain conditions to exist before I take action, this does not have to be the case. In the journey towards believing this, I may go back to my demand and wait for a so-called necessary condition to exist before I take action, but I can recognise these times and respond to them by challenging this rigid belief in thought and action.

Thus, I will oscillate between believing that certain conditions are necessary to motivate me to act and believing that these conditions are desirable, but not necessary. My goal is not to eradicate my demand, but to minimise its impact by noticing when I make it and counteracting it in thought and deed.

So what are the advantages and disadvantages of a realistic rational self-motivation credo? I first discussed the advantages and disadvantages of holding such a credo in Chapter 2. Applying these to the realistic rational self-motivation credo presented above, we may say the following. Its advantages seem to be:

1 It gives people a warts-and-all picture of rational self-motivation that is within the grasp of most people.
2 Even though periods of irrational thinking and unhealthy action are present in realistic rational self-motivation, there is still a clear indication of the rational thinking that people should aim for.
3 It can comfort those people who value realism in their quest for greater self-motivation.

However, there are disadvantages to the realistic rational self-motivation credo:

1 It may legitimise disturbance and unhealthy action as necessary components of self-motivation, whereas, in reality, they are frequently rather than inevitably occurring components.
2 It may discourage those people who are capable of a more ideal form of self-motivation (i.e. one relatively free from disturbance and unhealthy action).

However, in my view the advantages of this credo outweigh its disadvantages and, given its realistic nature, it is useful for a person to apply it when seeking to motivate themselves.

Motivation is an important factor in the development and maintenance of self-discipline which is the topic of the next chapter.

Chapter 7

Self-discipline

Introduction

'What I need is greater self-discipline!' How many times have you heard that? Well there is good news and bad news.

First, the good news. A person can learn to become more self-disciplined. This is true even if the person thinks that she is completely undisciplined. The bad news is that becoming more self-disciplined is not easy. I wish it was, but generally it is not. Indeed, developing greater self-discipline is something of a paradox, in that a person needs to be disciplined in order to become more self-disciplined. But enough of the problems and technicalities. Let me consider what self-discipline is. I believe that if a person knows what self-discipline is, then this will help her to develop it. So, I will consider the concept of self-discipline and look carefully at its five components.

Dryden's definition of self-discipline

The following is my definition of self-discipline:

> A person is self-disciplined (a) when she has decided to work towards longer-term goals to which she has chosen to commit herself and to forgo shorter-term goals that are obstacles to achieving these longer-term goals, *and* (b) when she acts on this decision. When the person is self-disciplined she acknowledges that there is a part of her that wishes to pursue these shorter-term goals, but she is able to stand back and choose to pursue what is in her own best interests.

This definition incorporates the five components of self-discipline. Thus:

- Component 1: *Improvement* (my definition mentions longer-term goals to which the person has chosen to commit herself).
- Component 2: *'Long-term self'* (my definition mentions a part of the person that has decided to work towards longer-term goals and that takes action in the service of these goals).
- Component 3: *'Short-term self'* (my definition mentions a part of the person that wishes to pursue these shorter-term goals).
- Component 4: *'Executive self'* (my definition mentions a part of the person that is able to stand back and choose to pursue what is in her own best interests).
- Component 5: *Obstacles* (my definition mentions shorter-term goals that are obstacles to achieving these longer-term goals).

I will now discuss these five components in greater detail.

Improvement

If we consider the concept of improvement, we will see that it is a general term that suggests a state that is healthy or good for the person. Broadly speaking, such a state enhances a person's well-being (physical, psychological and, if relevant, spiritual). If the person has not achieved such a state then their achievement is usually in the longer term and, generally, they have to expend effort and/or deny themselves pleasure to achieve it. For example, if it is healthy for a woman to weigh 147 lbs and she currently weighs 167 lbs then the achievement of the healthy state lies in the future and involves the woman denying herself pleasure (i.e. she needs to refrain from eating high-calorie tasty foodstuffs) and the expenditure of effort (if exercise plays a part in her weight loss programme).

Who defines the person's goals?

This raises the question of who defines what is healthy or good for the person. The person will increase the chances of being self-disciplined if she, herself, defines what is healthy or good for her. If others define this and she disagrees with them, then her motivation to pursue this so-called 'healthy' or 'good' state will be quite low (see Chapter 6). Indeed, if the person is what psychologists call 'reactant' (meaning highly sensitive to having her sense of autonomy threatened), then she will not pursue this state precisely because others have defined it as productive for her, even if she agrees with them.

However, even if the person does decide what is healthy or good for her, this is not, on its own, sufficient to promote self-discipline.

Making a commitment to seek improvement

A commonly heard phrase is 'I know I should get down to work . . .' What a statement like this signifies is that the person knows what is good for her, but does not act on it. What is missing here is a statement indicating that the person is making a commitment to pursue whatever it is that she has defined as being healthy for her. Committing herself to a sustained course of healthy action is important in the sense that when she does so, she decides to act on what she knows is healthy. Without such a commitment all the person does is acknowledge that a course of action is healthy, and this acknowledgement on its own very often does not lead to self-discipline.

Making a commitment to take a particular course of healthy action is important when the person is faced with a number of such courses of action, but she is unable or unwilling to follow all of them. In committing to a particular course of healthy action, the person is choosing among the available courses of action on offer and deciding to implement one.

Taking action

While making a commitment to follow a course of action is important, it is insufficient for the person to achieve her goals. Taking action is the only reliable way to achieve improvement. A commitment is a cognitive or thinking procedure, while taking action involves behaviour and it is only behaviour that will enable the person to achieve her longer-term goals.

Let me illustrate what I mean by discussing the writing of this book. For quite a while now, I have wanted to write a book on psychological health, but I have had a number of other projects to attend to. Once I had completed these projects I made a commitment to write this book. However, I had to act on this commitment and actually write 500 words a day (my writing regime involves writing 500 words every day) in order for me to achieve my goal. This is what I did and you are reading the results of my decision to act on my commitment to write this book.

When the person chooses not to take action in the service of her goals, but instead chooses to take some other action, it is important that she understands the factors in operation at that time. It may be that she finds the goal-related action uncomfortable, anxiety-provoking or anger-engendering, to give three examples.

Achievement vs. maintenance

When we think of goals we tend to think of their achievement. Thus, in the example that I discussed earlier, where a woman had to lose 20 lbs for health reasons, it is one thing to achieve the weight target of 147 lbs, it is quite another to maintain it. In general, while the achievement of any long-term goal that involves effort and/or restraint is difficult, it is much harder to maintain such gains. To do so, the person needs to make enduring changes in her behavioural repertoire. Let's assume that the woman altered her eating behaviour and lost 20 lbs, but when she did so, she immediately went back to her previous high-calorie diet. What would happen? Quite clearly she would put back on the weight that she had lost, and, in all probability, more quickly than it took her to lose it in the first place. So if a person wanted to maintain her weight at 147 lbs, she would have to make enduring changes in her eating habits from those that led to her problem in the first place.

Long-term self

What I have called the long-term self (LTS) is the part of the person that is entrusted with the task of looking after her long-term healthy interests from a psychological, physical and, if relevant, spiritual perspective. When fulfilling this task, the long-term self is ever mindful of the longer term rather than the shorter term. The person's LTS is the part of her that reminds her that there are 'no gains, without pains' and 'if you want something, then you have to work for it'. This part of the person encourages her to make short-term sacrifices for long-term gains. Thus, it urges her to refrain from engaging in behaviours that are pleasurable, but self-defeating in the longer term. It reminds her of her healthy long-term goals and that the effort that she needs to expend to achieve them is worth it.

Again, when doing its job correctly, the person's LTS shows her that she, as a person, is worth making sacrifices for. It is therefore also concerned with encouraging the person to preserve and act on a healthy attitude towards herself (see Chapter 5).

Short-term self

The short-term self (STS) is concerned with satisfying a person's basic instincts. It is not at all concerned with her longer-term healthy interests. Its motto might be said to be: 'Eat, drink and be merry for tomorrow we might die.' As such it is the part of the person that is her own biggest block to developing self-discipline.

The short-term self is not only concerned with pleasure; it is also concerned with the relief of pain and discomfort in their broadest sense.

Fortunately, it is rare that a person is completely dominated by her short-term self, but when this happens, it has catastrophic results. Many years ago, I attended a case conference in Manhattan. The person whom we were considering was a 32-year-old man who had inherited vast wealth. He was obese, very unfit and spent a considerable amount of money each week paying people to do basic chores for him: cleaning his apartment, preparing his food, washing him and even cleaning his teeth! The question we were asked to address in the case conference was: should the therapist, who was being asked to take on this person as a client, go to his apartment to carry out therapy or not, given that the client would not come to the therapist's office? The person was miserable, but wouldn't do anything to help himself because he was dominated by his short-term self.

Executive self

The fifth and final component of self-discipline is what I call the executive self (ES). This is the part of a person that mediates between the long-term and short-term selves. It helps to ensure that the person has a healthy balance in life between pursuing her longer-term goals and satisfying her shorter-term goals. This dispels a common misconception that the major task of the executive self is to ensure that the long-term self is in control. While this is the case to some degree (as shown in the general dictionary definitions of self-discipline), if this were exclusively the case then the person would only be pursuing her longer-term goals and she would have no short-term fun. This would be like putting money in a savings account and never spending any of it.

On the other hand, if the person's STS were in the driving seat then this would be like spending everything she had (and probably getting into debt too) and saving nothing. The task of the executive self is to make sure that the person makes an investment in her future and that she pursues short-term enjoyment – in other words, that she lives a balanced life rather than one of either austerity or profligacy. The ES is at its most efficient when it helps the person to attend to her long-term self before attending to her short-term self rather than vice versa, although exceptions to this 'rule' are permitted.

Obstacles: What they are and how to address them effectively

The path towards self-discipline is filled with obstacles that need to be addressed and overcome. In this section, I will discuss obstacles that prevent people from taking self-disciplined action and those that lead them to take self-undisciplined action. There are many things that a person can engage in which serve as obstacles to self-discipline in the sense that this engagement interferes with her pursuing her long-term self-disciplined goals. These things tend to be pleasurable or less aversive than the activities that would lead to goal achievement.

However, it is not the presence of these obstacles that lead to people to self-indiscipline, but the rigid beliefs that they hold about these obstacles and the actions they take based on these rigid beliefs. I will discuss two types of these rigid beliefs: i) those that relate to the conditions that people believe have to exist before they take self-disciplined action and ii) those that relate to urges to engage in self-undisciplined behaviour that lead them to "give in" to these urges.

Rigid beliefs about pre-action conditions: The biggest obstacle that prevents people from taking self-disciplined action

The biggest block to implementing a commitment to longer-term, self-disciplined goals that involve taking action, concerns the conditions that the person believes have to exist before she takes such action. In reality, while the presence of these conditions may be desirable they certainly don't have to exist before the person takes action towards her self-disciplined goals. In other words, the person can take action even though these conditions are absent. Here is a list of commonly expressed 'necessary' conditions:

- Motivation
- Anxiety or Pressure
- Confidence
- Competence
- Certainty
- External control
- Self-control
- Full comprehension
- Comfort
- Favourable external conditions.

It is important that the person does the following if she wants to free herself from the constraints of rigid beliefs concerning these conditions:

- identify the existence of such a rigid belief
- question it and respond to it with its flexible alternative
- take action while holding the flexible belief when the condition is not present
- accept that taking action in the absence of the desired condition goes against the comfortable grain.

Rigid beliefs about urges: The biggest obstacle that prevents people refraining from taking self-undisciplined action

In refraining-based self-discipline, a person is called upon to deal with urges to engage in immediate pleasurable activities which go counter to the pursuit of her self-disciplined goals. In biblical terms, her task in this area is to 'yield not to temptation' unless doing so has been incorporated into her overall self-disciplined plan (e.g. having a planned bar of chocolate as part of a calorie controlled diet). However, in this section, I will assume that acting on such urges is not part of such a plan.

In order to deal with an urge, the person needs to understand what it is. An urge is a strong, often viscerally-based tendency to engage in a pleasurable activity or to rid oneself of a negative state.

If a person holds a rigid belief about such urges then she will 'yield' to temptation or act on her urges and thus set herself back in developing greater self-discipline. Acting in ways that are consistent with flexible alternatives to these rigid beliefs forms a central part of dealing effectively with such urges as will now be shown.

Coping with urges

Here are the steps that a person needs to take in order to deal effectively with such urges.

Acknowledge the presence of the urge

If a person does not acknowledge that she is experiencing an urge, then she is likely to act on it. So she needs to admit to herself that she is tempted to do something that is not in her long-term interests to do.

Acknowledge that it is not necessary to act on the urge immediately

This step is particularly important in that it involves the person rehearsing the rational belief that she does not have to act on the urge straightaway even though she wants to. Breaking what might be called the urge-action fusion is particularly important in coping with urges.

Recognise the presence of choice: To act on the urge or not

Once the person has shown herself that she does not have to act on her urge, she is then in a position to recognise that she can choose to act on her urge or to refrain from doing so. As I noted earlier, self-discipline does not just involve acting in accord with long-term self-disciplined goals; rather it involves paying attention to these goals while ensuring that some short-term goals are met. Thus, a person may choose to act on her urge if doing so does not interfere with her developing self-discipline.

*Review the positive reasons for refraining from acting on
the urges and the negative reasons for acting on them*

If the person has chosen to refrain from acting on her urge or if
she is still debating whether or not to do so, then she may benefit
from reviewing the reasons why it is in her interests to refrain from
acting on her urge and why it is not in her interests to act on
the urge.

*Respond to any 'positive' reasons for acting on an urge
and to any 'negative' reasons against refraining from
doing so*

While reviewing the pros and cons of acting on her urge and of
refraining from doing so, the person may discover pros for acting
on them and cons against refraining from doing so. If she does, it is
important that she responds to such reasons so that she neutralises
their effect on her behaviour or decision-making.

Take purposive action even the urge is still present

If the person has decided to refrain from acting on her urge then it
is important that she gets on with what she would be doing if she
did not experience the urge. She needs to do this even though she
experiences the urge. If she does this then she will discover, in all
probability, that the intensity of her urge will initially increase,
since she is not satisfying it, but then it will decrease.

Once the person has taken such steps to deal with her urges, she
will discover which are the most powerful and which can be de-
emphasized in her ongoing struggle to deal effectively with
'temptation'.

A credo for self-discipline based on rational beliefs and realism

In this final section, I will outline what I call a realistic rational self-
discipline credo. This is comprised of a set of beliefs which promote
realistic self-discipline in the face of temptation and discomfort. I
will put this credo in the first person and as you read it bear in
mind that it is a general credo which needs to be applied to specific
situations which call for a self-disciplined response.

As a human being I recognise that I have short-term desires for pleasure and freedom from discomfort and longer-term desires which require self-discipline to achieve. When I am faced with a choice between fulfilling these two sets of desires, I will tend to favour fulfilling the short-term desires. At times I will believe that I have to have what I want immediately or that I have to get rid of what I don't want straight away. Sometimes I will act on these demands, but at those times I also have the capacity to notice when I am about to do so and to stand back and do the following. I can remind myself that while I want to have what I want or get rid of what I don't want, there is no reason why I have to have either set of conditions and I can tolerate the deprivation and discomfort of not having my desires met, particularly when it is worth it to me to do so. So I can remind myself what my longer-term goals are at this point and recognise that I can act in a self-disciplined way to achieve these goals. Thus, I can refrain from acting to satisfy short-term temptation and I can begin to do things that I would rather not do when doing so will help me to achieve my self-disciplined goals.

I recognise that it is a real struggle for me to maintain self-discipline and that sometimes I will transform my desires into demands and act to satisfy those demands in self-undisciplined ways. However, I can learn from these experiences without condemning myself and renew my commitment to be self-disciplined.

In the journey towards self-discipline, I may well deceive myself and give myself so-called good reasons why I acted in a self-undisciplined manner. However, I can learn to spot these rationalisations, to keenly differentiate them from legitimate reasons and to respond healthily to my attempts at self-deceit. Thus, I can use rationalisations as a cue to think rationally about temptations on the one hand and discomfort on the other. While I recognise that I can do this, I also acknowledge that there will be times when I won't. The path towards greater self-discipline is a rocky one. When I do eventually think rationally about temptations and discomfort, I will accept that when I don't get my desires met, I will feel badly about this, even though I have acknowledged that I don't have to get what I want. These bad feelings are healthy. They are a sign that I have desires, that these desires are not being met and they motivate me to act in self-disciplined ways. However, I also recognise that it is very difficult for me to have desires about dealing with temptation and discomfort and to keep these desires flexible. As such, I will return to disturbed negative feelings when I go back to holding rigid demands and, on these occasions, I recognise that I am particularly vulnerable to acting in self-undisciplined ways.

I also recognise that when I don't satisfy my immediate desires and experience discomfort, I tend to think that it is awful and the end of the world when this happens. When I do so, I cannot see any good in what is happening or acknowledge that there are other things in life that are important to me. It is a real struggle for me to accept that when I don't satisfy my immediate desires, this is bad and unfortunate but not terrible or the end the world. I can believe this, but I will oscillate between thinking in this way and thinking that it's awful to be deprived until I make the former stronger than the latter. This will be interspersed with attempts to use rationalisations to justify my 'giving into temptation and delivering myself from discomfort'. When I do eventually operate according to my non-awfulising belief, I will be in a better frame of mind to acknowledge that good can come from bad and even when I choose not to meet my strongest, immediate desires. I have other longer-term, self-disciplined goals that I can strive to meet.

I also recognise that when I am faced with temptation or discomfort and I demand that I have to get what I want or be free of what I don't want then I tend to think that it is unbearable when this happens and that I will never be happy again. It is again a real struggle for me to accept that when my desires about temptation and discomfort are not met, this is bearable and that I can bear it. I realise that I can believe this, but I will oscillate between believing that I can bear it and believing that I can't until I make the former stronger than the latter. This will again be interspersed with attempts to justify my self-undisciplined behaviour in order that I quickly get what I want or quickly get rid of my disturbed feelings. When I do believe that I can bear putting up with the discomfort of not having what I want, I am in a better frame of mind to see that I do not lose my capacity for happiness when temptation and discomfort do occur and can gain such happiness in other areas of my life, if not now, then at some point in the not too distant future.

If I act in a self-undisciplined manner either because I have to get what I want or because I have to get rid of what I don't want, I tend to depreciate myself and find it a real struggle to acknowledge that I am a fallible human being equal in worth to all other human beings although we differ in a myriad of different respects. I can eventually do this, but recognise that I will oscillate between depreciating myself and accepting myself, interspersed with rationalisations, until I make my self-acceptance belief stronger than my self-depreciation belief. When I do this I can see that this belief will help me to stand back and accept myself for lapsing and that I can learn from these experiences so that I can move towards greater self-discipline.

While flexible and non-extreme beliefs will help me to develop self-discipline, I recognise that even when I work hard to develop such beliefs, I will often return to thinking rigidly and in extreme ways. Similarly, I acknowledge that as I work to internalise this realistic credo, I will experience many lapses along the way. The best way of dealing with these lapses is to accept them, without liking them, learn specific things from them and act on such specific learning in relevant future situations.

When I do disturb myself about acting in self-undisciplined ways, I will struggle with that and may well disturb myself for thus disturbing myself. I will strive to accept myself for disturbing myself about failures to deal healthily with temptation and discomfort, and recognise that as I do so my efforts will oscillate between accepting myself, depreciating myself and various forms of denial. If I persevere, I will help my self-acceptance belief to gain ascendancy and, when this happens, I will acknowledge that while it is desirable that I do not disturb myself, I am not immune from doing so and nor do I have to be immune. However, I will struggle with this too and at times will go back to demanding that I must not disturb myself about failing to act in self-disciplined ways. Once I have largely accepted myself for disturbing myself, I can then work on the original disturbance and only then, when I have done this relatively successfully, will I attempt to deal more healthily with threats to self-discipline. If I attempt to become more self-disciplined while I am feeling disturbed or feeling disturbed about feeling disturbed, my attempts will be contaminated by my disturbed feelings and I will usually be less successful at becoming more self-disciplined. In fact, I may well make things more difficult for myself. However, being human I may well do the wrong thing and attempt to become more self-disciplined when I am disturbed in the first place and disturbed about being disturbed in the second place. The best I can do is to catch myself doing so and work on not doing so. My successes here will be punctuated by lapses, as before.

So what are the advantages and disadvantages of a realistic rational self-discipline credo? I first discussed the advantages and disadvantages of holding such a credo in Chapter 2. Applying these to the realistic rational self-discipline credo, we may say the following. Its advantages seem to be:

1   It gives people a warts-and-all picture of rational self-discipline that is within the grasp of most people.
2   Even though periods of irrational thinking and rationalisation are present in realistic rational self-discipline, there is still a clear indication of the rational thinking that people should aim for.
3   It can comfort rather than inspire and can thus motivate those people who value realism in their quest for greater self-discipline.

However, there are disadvantages to the realistic rational self-discipline credo:

1   It may legitimise disturbance and rationalisation as necessary components of self-discipline, whereas, in reality, they are frequently rather than inevitably occurring components.
2   It may discourage those people who are capable of a more ideal form of self-discipline (i.e. one relatively free from disturbance and rationalisation).

However, in my view the advantages of this credo outweigh its disadvantages and, given its realistic nature, it is useful for a person to apply it in his or her quest to become more self-disciplined.

In the following chapter, I will consider the topic of resilience.

Chapter 8

Resilience

Introduction

The concept of resilience has attracted much recent interest, but it is not always clear what writers mean by the concept. So, in this chapter, I will offer a personal view on what resilience is and what it is not.

A commonly found view of resilience sees it as involving:

1 The existence of a state of equilibrium in a person
2 Some kind of disruption to this existing state (e.g. a setback)
3 A quick return to the state that existed before the disruption occurred.

Such a view is problematic for a number of reasons.

1 It does not make clear what a disruption is

Is it something that happens to the person? This is implied by the word 'setback', but it is not clear. Is it the person's disrupted response to this event? This book is based on the ideas of Rational Emotive Behaviour Therapy (REBT), a form of cognitive behaviour therapy (CBT). In REBT, a situational ABC framework is used to help the person understand his (in this case) psychological response that occurs in a specific context – this is known as an 'emotional episode'. In that framework, we have the following components:

1 The situation or context in which the person's response occurs.
2 'A' stands for the aspect of the situation to which the person responds. This event may be an actual aspect of the situation or an inference that the person makes about the situation.
3 'B' stands for the beliefs a person holds about this event.

4 'C' stands for the consequences of holding these beliefs about the event (Dryden and Branch, 2008). These consequences are best seen as the person's responses to the event mediated or influenced as they are by the beliefs that the person holds about the event.

Now when the term 'disruption' is considered in the context of resilience, such disruption can occur at 'A', where the event (real or inferred) has disrupted a person's state of equilibrium, and it can occur at 'C', where the person's emotions and/or behaviour show signs of disruption. The common view of resilience does not make this subtle distinction.

I will consider REBT's view of resilience later in this chapter.

2 It does not allow for the fact that the pre-disruption state may be unhealthy

The common view of resilience also implies that the state that the person was in before the disruption occurred was not unhealthy. Thus, it talks about returning to 'shape' which, while this term is vague, does conjure up a 'not unhealthy' state of affairs. It does not consider, therefore, that this 'shape' may be unhealthy, i.e. that the person may already have been in an unhealthy state before the disruption occurred.

3 It does not consider the specificity of the disruption at 'A'

Even when a disruption occurs at 'A', the common view of resilience does not make clear how specific the 'setback' is. It does not allow us to distinguish between what may be called situational resilience (the person's ability to respond resiliently to *a particular setback at 'A'*) and trait resilience (the person's general ability to respond resiliently to *general setbacks at 'A'*). A number of things can disrupt a person's equilibrium which dictionary definitions do not, in general, consider, and I will discuss these now.

4 It does not differentiate between disruptions that can be changed and those that cannot be changed

The common view of resilience does not distinguish between disruptions at 'A' which can be changed and those that cannot be changed which thus call upon the person to make the necessary adjustments to this unchangeable disruption.

5 It does not distinguish between short-lived and enduring disruptions

The common view of resilience does not distinguish between short-lived disruptions at 'A' and more enduring disruptions. A resilient response may be different when the disruption is short-lived than when it is enduring.

6 It does not make clear whether or not a disrupted response is a necessary part of resilience

The common view of resilience does not make clear whether or not a disrupted response at 'C' is an essential part of resilience. It is *possible* for a person to respond resiliently to an adversity without such a disruption at 'C' occurring. Even if such disrupted responses are usual, how severe do they have to be for them to be considered a part of the process of resilience? Can a psychotic breakdown be a healthy part of resilience, as R.D. Laing, the controversial Scottish psychiatrist, would have argued decades ago? Flach (1997) has argued that breakdown (albeit not a schizophrenic one) is a healthy part of the resilience process. Furthermore, Flach would regard with scepticism a claim for resilience that did not involve some form of breakdown.

7 It implies that a return to the same state of equilibrium that existed before the negative event occurred is a defining feature of resilience

The common view of resilience seems to imply that the goal of resilience is a return to the same state of equilibrium that existed before the disruption occurred. If it is, this seems to rule out that the person can be changed for the better as a result of this experience. Surely, resilience allows for growth and development as a consequence of the person's encounter with the negative event? Indeed it could be argued that if the person was *not* changed for the better, then that person has not demonstrated resilience.

8 It expounds the myth of quickly bouncing back

Resilience-based behaviour in the face of adversity is often thought to be characterised by bouncing back from the adversity. I believe that this presents a false picture of resilience and even encourages what might be called resilience perfectionism where a person may expect himself to respond immediately to an adversity in a constructive manner, and if he departs from this ideal response he will get angry with himself for failing to respond in the right way to adversity.

Resilience misconception I: Resilience involves 'bouncing back'

Gerald came to counselling after he lost his wife to cancer. He was ashamed and angry with himself because he felt sad and listless two weeks after her death. When I asked him why he was ashamed he said that he should feel like going back to work by now and that death was a fact of life and he should be back to his 'normal' self by now. Gerald had the idea in his head that resilience was 'bouncing back' from adversity, and because he was not doing this (indeed, he was showing all the normal and healthy signs of grief), he considered himself to be a weak, self-indulgent person.

As I have just mentioned, I consider that the view of resilience which portrays it as involving a quick 'bouncing back' to a state of equilibrium that predated the adversity to be false and even dangerous, as people can disturb themselves over struggling back instead of the expected bouncing back. Instead, I see resilience as essentially involving pain and struggle. Let me concentrate on this for it is crucial to an understanding of psychological resilience.

9 It does not consider that resilience often involves emotional pain

In the previous section, I made the point that resilience involves the person experiencing negative emotions in the face of adversity. The common view of resilience does not cover this psychological reality. This point alone makes the view flawed, in my opinion. Particularly when the adversity is highly unpleasant, resilience will involve the person experiencing very painful emotions and when this happens the person will be sorely tempted to act in ways that eliminate or reduce this pain. If the person acts on these tendencies, he may well eliminate or reduce his emotional pain in the moment, but he will be storing up trouble for himself in that he will be implicitly teaching himself to avoid emotional pain as a way of coping with adversity. This rarely works in the long run and psychologists are increasingly realising that what some have called 'experiential avoidance' (Hayes and Strosahl, 2004) is a key ingredient of non-resilience as well as a major way in which people perpetuate their psychological problems. It follows, therefore, that what has come to be known as a 'willingness to experience' emotional pain, and acting in ways that embody this principle, is a major ingredient of resilience.

Resilience involves emotional pain: an example

Gerald, whom we met earlier on p. 123, came to recognise that it was not weak to grieve for his wife. He allowed himself to experience the pain of loss and decided to go back to work gradually. He asked his sister to come in a few times a week to teach him how to use the dishwasher and washing machine but he was determined to learn these new skills for himself. Whenever his grief was too much for him, he took time off work and asked for more help from his sister. After several months he was back at work full-time (with the occasional day off to grieve) and was doing all the chores that his late wife had done, with the help of his children who all pitched in to help their dad. Gerald still misses his wife terribly, but is looking forward to the future with optimism.

10 It does not consider that resilience often involves struggle

The idea that the person can quickly bounce back from adversity is based on an unrealistic idea of what it means to be strong psychologically. While resilience is characterised by strength, it is the nature of such strength that is in dispute not the concept of strength itself. A similar point can be made about bravery. When a person acts bravely he does not do so without fear; rather, he does so with fear. It is not easy to act bravely. It often involves a struggle. Part of the person wants to confront the threat that he is facing and part of the person wishes to avoid it or withdraw from it. The person can be said to act bravely when he ultimately acts on the former tendency rather than the latter.

The same is true when I consider resilient behaviour. When the person is in emotional pain in the face of adversity, part of the person wants to act to eliminate or reduce his pain and another part of him wants to deal productively with the adversity. The person is thus involved in a struggle that can be quite intense at times. The common view of resilience makes no reference to struggle being a part of resilience.

Resilience involves struggle: an example

Leanne is a recovering alcoholic and was regularly attending Alcoholics Anonymous (AA) meetings. She is a single woman who was beginning to get her life back together after the end of a long relationship, when she was made redundant from her job. Her AA colleagues were of tremendous support to her and, after going back home for two weeks to her parents who did not drink at all, Leanne returned to London to begin to look for a job. Every day was a struggle for her. Every day she wanted to drown her sorrows and some days she did. However, on most days she accepted her urge to drink, but instead of acting on the urge, she rang her AA sponsor, went to an AA meeting or listened to classical music until the urge passed. Despite this struggle, Leanne organised her days so that she was occupied full-time in finding a new job. She made numerous applications, attended many interviews and persisted when she was not offered the positions. Her persistence eventually paid off and six months after being made redundant, she began a new job.

In order to refrain from acting to rid himself of his emotional pain, the person needs a good reason for doing so (see Chapter 6). The common view of resilience, as I have noted, states that resilience involves the person returning to the state of equilibrium that he was in before this state was disrupted. I would disagree that returning to this state of equilibrium should be the prime reason for refraining from acting to reduce or eliminate psychological pain. There are two better reasons for exercising such restraint.

1 Exercising restraint is healthy

Acting on an urge to rid oneself of emotional pain will only help to perpetuate this pain in the longer run. Unless the person faces up to his pain and deals with it, he will be looking all the time for ways to avoid it. This will mean that he will limit himself by avoiding situations in which he might feel pain, and he may begin to develop a problem with drink, drugs or food, as he uses one or more of these to dull his pain. Facing up to his emotional pain will mean that he will not misuse the above-mentioned substances and he will be free to go where he wants.

It is healthy for a person to refrain from acting to rid himself of psychological pain: an example

Albert was involved in a road traffic accident that left him with a bad whiplash injury. After he came out of hospital, he began to develop flashbacks of the accident that he found very distressing. Every time he had the flashback, he experienced a strong urge to rid himself immediately of the associated distress. He began to drink after he had a flashback containing a painful image of the accident and soon developed a drink problem. He avoided driving and refused to enter the area in which the accident occurred. He also banned his family from mentioning any aspect of the accident or anything that reminded him of the accident. In trying to help himself, as he thought, by avoiding pain, Albert came to realise that he was only making himself worse. He had developed a drink problem and he was seriously restricting himself geographically. His GP referred him to a counsellor who helped him to see the value of facing up to his distress and of refraining from acting on his immediate urge to rid himself of this distress. This helped him to allow himself to experience the flashbacks and to process what happened to him in the accident in a way that enabled him eventually to move on with his life.

2 Exercising restraint helps the person to achieve his longer-term goals

When the person refrains from acting on his strong urge to get rid of or reduce his psychological pain he frees himself to pursue longer-term goals. The person will be more able to take healthy risks and focus his attention and his energy on pursuing these goals. Acting to rid himself of pain is very much a short-term goal and if the person prioritises pursuing this goal rather than his longer-term goals then he will be unfulfilled and living life defensively, always on the lookout to protect himself against psychological pain.

Refraining from acting to rid himself of psychological pain helps a person to achieve her goals: an example

Jan was a very talented singer whose major goal in life was to sing professionally. However, she suffered from performance anxiety which in her mind stopped her from pursuing this goal. She came to believe that she could only go for singing auditions when she had solved her problem, which for her meant singing without anxiety. While she was perfectly at ease during singing lessons and while singing for her family, she became anxious both before and during auditions and performances. As soon as she started feeling anxious, Jan would avoid the situation, the consequence being that she was beginning to acquire the reputation of someone who would routinely cancel or even fail to turn up for auditions.

Jan's parents asked if they could help by paying for counselling sessions for her, and she agreed to go. There she learned that she would have to confront her fears if she was to overcome them. Her counsellor helped her to see the self- and performance-defeating beliefs that underpinned her anxiety. She also taught Jan that if she was going to progress in her career as a singer, then she would have to tolerate her anxious feelings instead of trying to rid herself of them. Jan was helped to see that she could sing even though she was anxious and as she went forward with this in mind she began to be offered singing parts in quite prestigious productions.

11 It overlooks the resilience behaviour ratio

So far I have stressed that resilience involves pain and struggle. If the person accepts the idea that resilience involves struggle, he may erroneously think that he can only be resilient if he *always* wins the struggle and acts resiliently. I don't think that this is the case. I see resilience in the same way as I see concepts like self-esteem, self-discipline and self-actualisation (i.e. realising one's potential) – as goals to work towards, but which can never be perfectly achieved. It is best, therefore, to think in terms of striving to develop greater resilience.

Resilience, in my view, can best be seen as representing a ratio of healthy to unhealthy behaviour. The more healthily the person behaves in the face of adversity, the greater resilience he is demonstrating. Note then that resilience allows for the fact that, at times, the person may well lose the struggle and act in short-term protective but resilience-defeating ways. However, as long as his ratio is in credit (greater healthy to unhealthy behaviour) then the person is acting resiliently in the face of adversity. His goal then becomes to develop greater resilience and increase what I call his 'resilience behaviour ratio'. The common view of resilience does not allow for the existence of such a ratio.

The resilience behaviour ratio: an example

Kevin and Barbara were finding dealing with their two children very difficult. As a result their lives were very fraught, with the children ruling the roost. Things got so bad that they sought help from a child psychologist who quickly ascertained the nature of the problem. Kevin and Barbara were unwittingly reinforcing their children's bad behaviour by paying attention to it. The psychologist helped them to see the problem, taught them to ignore negative behaviour and reward positive behaviour and helped them to address the obstacles that they had with respect to implementing her suggestions. Kevin and Barbara implemented these suggestions about 75 per cent of the time and, although their parenting was not perfect in this respect, their family life over time became much more peaceful as the children's behaviour improved.

Conclusion

This analysis shows that the common view of resilience raises as many questions as it answers when it comes to understanding psychological resilience. I conclude from this that one cannot rely on this common view to understand resilience.

Now let's consider the concept of resilience using the insights from REBT.

Resilience using the REBT framework

In this section, I will use the ABC framework that I mentioned earlier to show how REBT helps us to understand resilience and in doing so I will assume that the event or life context that the person is facing is negative (although positive events, like winning the lottery, may also call for a resilient response) – see Table 7.

Table 7 The ABC framework

Situation = the context in which the person's response occurred
'A' = the aspect of the situation to which the person responded
'B' = beliefs
'C' = consequences (of the interaction of A and B)

Situation

The situation is the context in which the person's response occurs. It is descriptive in nature and can be reliably described by a group of objective observers.

'A' = activating event

An activating event (or 'A') is the aspect of the situation to which the person responds. An 'A' can be an actual event within the larger situation or an inference that the person makes about the situation. An inference is an interpretation of the situation that goes beyond the data at hand. It may be correct or incorrect, but needs testing against the available data. When 'A's' are actual events they can refer to a number of things and these are listed in Table 8.

Table 8 Different adversities at 'A'

- A specific negative event
- A number of specific negative events co-occurring
- A specific negative event which serves to be the 'straw that breaks the camel's back'
- A general negative state of affairs

When considering 'A's' it is important to bear in mind two questions, which, as I showed above, the common view of resilience does not seek to answer:

1 Can these adversities be changed or not?
2 Are these adversities short-lived or enduring?

Examples

1 *Adversity that can be changed*:
   Muriel received a warning letter from the council for hanging her washing on her balcony.
2 *Adversity that cannot be changed*:
   Bill was made redundant from his job when his company went bankrupt.
3 *Short-lived adversity*:
   Fred was suspended from his job for a month after an anonymous complaint was received about his conduct at work.
4 *Enduring adversity*:
   Harry was diagnosed with colon cancer.

'B' = beliefs

The common view of resilience that I have presented only refers to events that occur at 'A' (i.e. a setback) or responses that occur at 'C' (i.e. a quick recovery). It does not refer to what I consider to be the most important factor in resilience. This is 'B' which refers to the beliefs about the adversities that enable a person to respond resiliently to them or not. This is ultimately why the common view of resilience is deficient. It ignores what I call the heart of resilience – which is the person's belief system.

Beliefs can be held about oneself, others and the world. Resilience-based beliefs tend to be flexible and non-extreme in nature while beliefs that get in the way of resilient responding are rigid and extreme in nature (Dryden, 2009b). At the end of this chapter, I will present a broad realistic flexible belief system (which I refer to as a credo) that underpins general resilience and which can be adapted for use in responding resiliently to specific adversities.

'C' = Consequences

As I said earlier, 'C' factors are the responses that a person makes
to events at 'A' which are mediated by his beliefs at 'B'. There are
three major consequences of 'B' that are particularly relevant to an
understanding of resilience. These are emotions (emotional
consequences), behaviour (behavioural consequences) and thinking
(thinking consequences).

Emotions

Emotions can be positive in tone, negative in tone or the person
may lack emotion.

Resilience is not marked by an absence of emotion

A common misconception of resilience is that it is characterised by
stoicism, a response to adversity characterised by strength and
lacking emotion. Nothing could be further from the truth. Indeed,
absence of emotion is often a sign that a person has not properly
digested what has happened to him and bodes poorly for future
resilience. The only true way that a person can have an unemo-
tional response to what has happened to him is when he genuinely
cares nothing about what has occurred. Consider the situation
where I look outside my window and notice that a man has just
walked past. I have no emotions about this fact because it holds no
significance to me whatsoever. It is a neutral event. As I argued
above, adversities are negative in nature and thus to respond to
them without emotion is not healthy and is not a good example of
resilience.

Resilience misconception II: Resilience does not involve any emotion

Perry found his girlfriend in bed with his best friend. He had always
prided himself on his ability to handle difficult situations and left the
scene calmly and without emotion. A day later he wrote a letter to
his girlfriend breaking off their relationship. In the letter, he thanked
her for her support and stated that he hoped that she would be
happy. Perry's friends were impressed by his 'chilled' attitude.

However, a week later, Perry was arrested for a road rage incident when a woman who looked very much like his girlfriend stalled her car in front of him.

Resilience is not marked by positive emotion

Positive emotions tend to occur when good things happen to a person and when that person gets what he wants. Now when a person is called upon to be resilient, it is, as the common view of resilience makes clear, when his state of equilibrium has been disrupted – either by a specific negative event or series of negative events or by a more pervasive general negative context. In any of these cases, it is unrealistic to expect the person to experience a positive emotion. In a nutshell, it is not realistic for a person to feel good about something bad.

Resilience misconception III: Resilience involves positive emotion

Linda came home to find that her flat had been burgled. Susan, who shared the flat with Linda, was very upset, but Linda felt pleased that nothing of value was stolen. A week later, Linda went off sick from her job because she couldn't get up in the morning due to delayed shock.

Resilience is marked by negative emotion

If resilience is marked neither by an absence of emotion nor by positive emotion, it follows that it is marked by negative emotion. Put simply, since resilience occurs in the context of adversity, it is healthy or adaptive to feel bad when bad things happen to you. However, and this is a key point, since resilience depends on a person being flexible and fluid when he is responding resiliently to an adversity he is not therefore stuck in his negative feelings. They do not immobilise him. Indeed, they tend to motivate the person to change what he realistically can change and adjust constructively to what he cannot change. It follows from this that the person only needs to target negative emotions for change when they prevent him from taking constructive action or from making a constructive adjustment.

Resilience involves negative emotion: an example

Peter was rejected by his girlfriend. He cried for days and felt very sad, but a month later he was dating a new woman whom he met at a dinner party.

Behaviour

In this section, I will consider behavioural responses to adversity. I would argue that unless a person puts his resilient attitudes into practice then he cannot truly be said to be demonstrating resilience. Acting resiliently is literally resilience in action.

Action tendencies and overt behaviour

Any behaviour can be divided into a tendency to act and an overt action. This is a very important distinction since resilience often involves (a) refraining from doing what the person 'feels like' doing and (b) doing what the person doesn't 'feel like' doing.

The difference between an action tendency and an overt behaviour: an example

I (WD) struggle with my weight and have a tendency to snack between meals which if left unchecked would lead to me putting on weight. When I am at a party and waitresses bring round canapés, the following dialogue often ensues.

Waitress: Would you like a canapé?
Windy: Yes, but I am not going to have one.

My response shows that I have a tendency towards taking a canapé based on my desire (I like canapés and if I could eat them without putting on weight, raising my blood pressure and my cholesterol levels, then I would) and my overt action (not taking a canapé and moving away from the waitress).

This difference between an action tendency and an overt behaviour is an important one. A realistic view of resilience states that resilience is based more on a person not converting a self-defeating action tendency into overt behaviour than it is on the absence of this action tendency.

Thinking

When thinking is the product of a person's beliefs about an adversity then this 'subsequent thinking', as I call it, is likely to be inferential in nature. When it stems from flexible rational beliefs this subsequent thinking tends to be balanced and realistic in nature while when it stems from rigid irrational beliefs, it tends to be heavily skewed to the negative and highly distorted in nature. Since resilience involves struggle, the person who is striving to react in a resilient manner may experience both types of subsequent thinking as they swing from holding flexible to holding rigid beliefs and back again until they eventually hold the former rather than the latter. I will discuss this point at the end of the chapter.

Dryden's definition of resilience

Based on all of the issues that I have discussed in this chapter, I will now put forward my own working definition of resilience. I will first present my view and then discuss its component parts.

What is resilience?

Resilience comprises a set of flexible cognitive, behavioural and emotional responses to acute or chronic adversities that can be unusual or commonplace. These responses can be learned and are within the grasp of everyone. While many factors affect the development of resilience, the most important one is the belief that the person holds about the adversity. Therefore, belief is the heart of resilience.

Resilience, as commonly understood, refers to 'bouncing back' from difficult experiences. A more detailed and realistic understanding of resilience involves the person frequently experiencing pain and struggle while 'coming back' rather than 'bouncing back' from misfortune. This experience of pain and struggle does not stop the person from working to change those adversities that can be changed and from adjusting constructively to those that cannot be changed. Nor does the experience of pain and struggle stop the person from moving towards his goals, however slowly, or pursuing what is important to him. This forward movement is a defining feature of resilience. As such, resilience does not restore the status quo in the person's life before the adversity occurred. Rather, what the person has learned changes him for the better and helps him to become more acutely aware of what is important in his life, and, as I have said, it encourages him to pursue it.

While resilience is the response of the person as an individual, its development can be facilitated or impaired by the context in which he lives, such as, respectively, having supportive friends or experiencing violent abuse from his partner, and thus is best understood within this context.

Here are the components of my view of resilience.

1 Resilience comprises a set of flexible cognitive, behavioural and emotional responses

There is nothing mystical about resilience. It can be explained with reference to psychological processes – cognitive (or thinking), emotional and behavioural – that are flexible in nature.

2 Resilience can occur in response to acute or chronic adversities that can be unusual or commonplace

It is a popular view of resilience that it mainly occurs in response to dramatic, catastrophic events. Common discussions of resilience specifically mention people's responses to the events that happened in the USA on September 11, 2001. Newspaper accounts of resilience more often than not focus on resilience in the face of unusual events, both acute (i.e. dramatic events that are time-bound, like 9/11 or a tsunami) and chronic (i.e. long-lasting events like the imprisonment of the Austrian girl who was held captive for many years).

While it is true that people can and often do respond resiliently to unusual acute or chronic adversities, it is very important not to

overlook resilience in the face of adversities that are more commonplace since this is the experience of most of us.

3 These responses can be learned and are within the grasp of everyone

These are two very important points. First, it is encouraging for
people to discover that they can *learn* to become resilient, that
resilience is not just the province of those fortunate enough to be
born with hardy genes. While people are born with different
temperaments, with some people responding more naturally in a
resilient way to adversities than others, everyone can learn to
become more resilient. Learning resilience means practice, so while
reading a book on how to become more resilient, for example, can
be the first step along the path to greater resilience, it is important
that the person recognises that he needs to put into practice what
he reads in such a book if he is truly to learn it.

4 Belief is the heart of resilience

The well-known Stoic philosopher, Epictetus, once famously said
that people are not disturbed by events, but by their views of
events. I think that these 'views' are best seen as representing
people's beliefs and thus I would say that the person's resilient
response at 'C' (in the ABC framework discussed above) to adversities at 'A' is dependent on his belief at 'B'.

5 Resilience does not mean 'bouncing back' from difficult experiences – rather, it involves the person experiencing pain and struggle as they come back from misfortune

I have mentioned a number of times in this chapter that a popular
conception of resilience is that it involves the person 'bouncing
back' from adversity. The concept of 'bouncing back' conjures up
an image of a quick and easy return to a previous state. I prefer to
talk of 'coming back' from misfortune which can and often does
involve pain and struggle and in a way that involves learning from
the experience rather than returning to the previous pre-adversity
state. As I said in my definition: 'what the person has learned
changes him for the better and helps him to become more acutely

aware of what is important in his life and . . . encourages him to
pursue it'.

6 Moving forward is a defining feature of resilience

While I stress that emotional pain and struggle very frequently
accompany resilience, I also stress that this pain and struggle does
not stop the person from pursuing his goals and addressing the
obstacles that might interfere with goal achievement. Hence, resilience helps the person to move forward and is one of its defining
features.

7 Resilience changes the person for the better

Rather than returning the person to the state that he was in before
the adversity occurred, I stress that it changes the person for the
better and helps him to become more aware of what his life's goals
are and the importance of actively pursuing them.

8 Resilience is best understood within the context in which it occurs

While it is true that resilience is demonstrated by individuals, it is
also true that the context in which it occurs is also important and,
therefore, if the person wishes to develop resilience he needs to pay
attention to contextual factors (external) as well as factors within
himself (internal).

My definition of resilience should, however, best be regarded as
a work in progress, rather than fixed in stone, since, like resilience
itself, a good definition of resilience should be flexible and promote
change.

A realistic rational resilience credo

In this final section, I will outline what I call a realistic rational
resilience credo. This is comprised of a set of beliefs which promote
realistic resilient responsiveness in the face of adversity. I will put
this credo in the first person and as you read it bear in mind that it
is a general credo which needs to be applied to specific adversities.

As a human being I recognise that I have many desires. I prefer certain conditions to exist in my life and other conditions not to exist. Particularly when faced with life's adversities, I tend to demand that the conditions that I want must exist and the conditions that I don't want must not exist. It is a real struggle for me to acknowledge that no matter how strong my desires are, sadly and regretfully, this does not mean that I have to have my desires met by myself, by others or by life conditions. In the journey towards believing this, I may well do many things to deal with my disturbed feelings which may help me in the short term, but not in the long term. Thus, I may deny that I feel disturbed and say either that I am not bothered about what happened or that I am handling it well. However, I recognise that denial is not healthy and will use this as a cue to think rationally about life's adversities as soon as I am able. While I recognise that I can do this, I also acknowledge that there will be times when I won't. The path towards greater resilience is a rocky one. When I do eventually think rationally about life's adversities, I will accept that when I don't get my desires met, I will feel badly about this, even though I have acknowledged that I don't have to get what I want. These bad feelings are healthy. They are a sign that I have desires, that these desires are not being met and they motivate me to change things if they can be changed and to adjust constructively if they can't be changed. However, I also recognise that it is very difficult for me to have desires about life conditions and to keep these desires flexible. As such, I will return to disturbed negative feelings when I go back to holding rigid demands.

I also recognise that when life's adversities occur and my desires are not met, I tend to think that it is awful and the end of the world when this happens. When I do so, I cannot see any good in what is happening or acknowledge that there are other things in life that are important to me. It is a real struggle for me to accept that when my desires about life's adversities are not met, this is bad and unfortunate but not terrible or the end the world. I can believe this, but I will oscillate between thinking in this way and thinking it is awful until I make the former stronger than the latter. This will be interspersed with attempts to deny that I feel disturbed about what happened. When I do eventually operate according to my non-awfulising belief,

I will be in a better frame of mind to acknowledge that good can come from bad and even when my strongest desires are not met, I have other desires that can be met, if not now, then at some time in the future.

I also recognise that when life's adversities occur and my desires are not met, I tend to think that it is unbearable when this happens and that I will never be happy again. It is again a real struggle for me to accept that when my desires about life's adversities are not met, this is bearable and that I can bear it. I realise that I can believe this, but I will oscillate between believing that I can bear it and believing that I can't until I make the former stronger than the latter. This will be again interspersed with attempts to deny that I feel disturbed about what happened in order that I quickly get rid of my disturbed feelings. When I do believe that I can bear adversities, I am in a better frame of mind to see that I do not lose my capacity for happiness when they do occur and can gain this in other areas of my life, if not now, then at some point in the not so distant future.

In the face of life's adversities which I have brought about, I tend to depreciate myself and find it a real struggle to acknowledge that I am a fallible human being equal in worth to all other human beings although we differ in a myriad of different respects. I can eventually do this, but recognise that I will oscillate between depreciating myself and accepting myself, interspersed with denial, until I make my self-acceptance belief stronger than my self-depreciation belief. When I do this I can see that this belief will help me to stand back and identify aspects of myself that I don't like and want to change. I will work steadily to change those negative aspects of myself that can be changed, and for those that I cannot change, I will attempt to do my best to minimise their impact. In striving to do this, I realise that I will often go back to depreciating myself and even when I basically accept myself I will occasionally depreciate myself.

In the face of life's adversities when others are responsible for them, I tend to depreciate them and find it very difficult to acknowledge that they are fallible human beings who will sadly often do the wrong thing and, equally sadly, fail to learn from their errors. I can believe this and will work towards doing so, but this is a real struggle for me because I easily condemn them and 'feel' powerful and justified in doing so. As I strive to accept others, I will often oscillate between depreciating them and accepting them, with periods of denial. When my other-acceptance belief is stronger than my other-depreciation belief, I can see that others acting badly is just the way they are and that as such they are fallible and not condemnable for their behaviour even if that behaviour is heinous.

In the face of life's adversities I tend to depreciate the whole of life and really struggle to accept that life is a complex mixture of the good, the bad and the neutral. When I do attain such acceptance, with the usual oscillations between life-acceptance, life-depreciation and denial in the face of highly aversive events, which may not be until a considerable amount of time has passed, then, I will see that the existence of highly aversive events does not change the complexity of life. The complexity of life incorporates highly aversive events, joyful events as well as many neutral events.

While flexible and non-extreme beliefs will help me to develop resilience, I recognise that even when I work hard to develop such beliefs, I will often return to thinking rigidly and in extreme ways. Similarly, I acknowledge that as I work to internalise this realistic credo, I will experience many lapses along the way. The best way of dealing with these lapses is to accept them, without liking them, learn specific things from them and act on such specific learning in relevant future situations.

When I do disturb myself about life's adversities, I will struggle with that and may well disturb myself for thus disturbing myself. I will strive to accept myself for disturbing myself about life's adversities, and I recognise that as I do so my efforts will oscillate between accepting myself, depreciating myself and various forms of denial. If I persevere, I will help my self-acceptance belief to gain ascendancy and, as this happens, I will acknowledge that while it is desirable that I do not disturb myself, I am not immune from doing so and nor do I have to be immune. However, I will struggle with this too and at times will go back to demanding that I must not disturb myself about life's adversities. Once I have largely accepted myself for disturbing myself, I can then work on the original disturbance and only then, when I have done this relatively successfully, will I attempt to change the adversities. If I attempt to change the adversities while I am feeling disturbed or disturbed about feeling disturbed, my attempts will be contaminated by my disturbed feelings and I will usually be less successful at changing the adversities. In fact, I may well make things more difficult for myself. However, being human I may well do the wrong thing and attempt to change the adversity when I am disturbed in the first place and disturbed about being disturbed in the second place. The best I can do is to catch myself doing so and work on not doing so. My successes here will be punctuated by lapses, as before.

So what are the advantages and disadvantages of a realistic rational resilience credo? I first discussed the advantages and disadvantages of holding such a credo in Chapter 2. Applying these to the realistic rational resilience credo presented above, we may say the following.

The advantages of this credo seem to be:

1   It gives people a warts-and-all picture of rational resilience that is within the grasp of most people.
2   Even though periods of irrational thinking and denial are present in realistic rational resilience, there is still a clear indication of the rational thinking that people should aim for.
3   It can comfort rather than inspire and can thus motivate those people who value realism in their quest for greater personal resilience.

However, there are disadvantages to the realistic rational resilience credo. These are:

1   It may legitimise disturbance and denial as necessary components of resilience, whereas, in reality, they are frequently rather than inevitably occurring components.
2   It may discourage those people who are capable of a more ideal form of resilience (i.e. one relatively free from disturbance and denial).

However, in my view the advantages of this credo outweigh its disadvantages and, given its realistic nature, it is useful for a person to apply it in dealing resiliently with specific adversities.

In the next chapter, I will consider the issue of tolerance of uncertainty.

Chapter 9

Tolerance of uncertainty

Introduction

It is a truism to say that we live in an uncertain world. By uncertainty, I mean the state where we do not know what has happened in the past, what is happening in the present or what will happen in the future. Let me briefly illustrate these three situations. An example of past uncertainty is when Mary lost her cat several years ago and doesn't know what happened to the pet. An example of present uncertainty is when a smoke alarm goes off in Peter's place of work and he does not know why. Finally, an example of future uncertainty is when Bob's firm announces a large cut in the workforce and he doesn't know whether or not he will lose his job. The position that I take in this book is that we can best deal with the uncertainties of life by adopting a set of flexible and non-extreme beliefs about them. I have outlined these beliefs in Chapters 2–5.

When we disturb ourselves about life's uncertainties, we don't disturb ourselves about the state of uncertainty itself. We disturb ourselves when we link uncertainty with another important aspect of our personal domain. Thus, in the examples that I provided above, Mary might have disturbed herself about the uncertainty concerning the *loss of her cat*, Peter might disturb himself about the uncertainty concerning *a possible threat to his life* and Bob might disturb himself about the uncertainty concerning the *possible loss of his livelihood*.

As such, I will not deal with how we can constructively deal with uncertainty on its own. Rather, I will consider how we can constructively respond when uncertainty is linked to some other aspect of our personal domain, and this other aspect usually involves some kind of 'threat'.

Dealing healthily with threat-based uncertainty

The best way to show you how to deal healthily with threat-based uncertainty is to compare a healthy response with an unhealthy response. I will first outline the unhealthy response and then compare this with a healthy way to respond to the same threat-based uncertainty.

Worry

When we worry we think we are facing an uncertainty-related threat, about which we hold a set of irrational beliefs. These beliefs then lead us (a) to feel anxious or worried, (b) to produce highly distorted thinking which we consider reflects imminent reality, and (c) to act in ways that are designed to keep us safe, but which in the longer term maintain the irrational beliefs underpinning our worry. It follows that we need to hold a set of rational beliefs about the uncertainty-related threat. This will enable us (a) to feel concerned, but not worried, (b) to produce realistic thinking which reflects the probable nature of what is going on, and (c) to act in ways that reflect probability.

Let me illustrate this by showing how two women handled the same uncertainty-related threat.

Maggie

Maggie was sitting in her lounge waiting for her teenage daughter to come home. Her daughter had said that she would be home by 8.30 pm and it was now 8.50 pm. Maggie had rung her daughter's mobile phone and got her voicemail. Maggie was very worried about not knowing whether or not her daughter was safe. She was worried because she held a set of irrational beliefs about threat-related uncertainty which had a number of effects that are characteristic of worry. Here is an 'ABC' analysis of Maggie's worry.

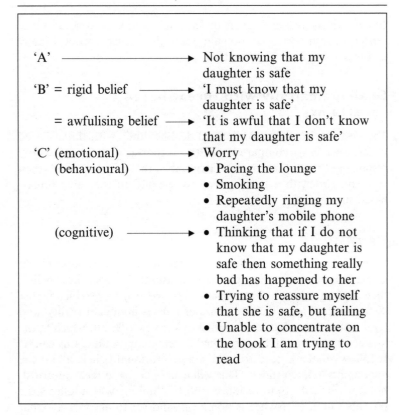

Veronica

Veronica was also sitting in her lounge waiting for her teenage daughter to come home. Her daughter had also said that she would be home by 8.30 pm and it was now 8.50 pm. Like Maggie, Veronica had rung her daughter's mobile phone and got her voicemail. However, unlike Maggie, Veronica was healthily concerned, but not worried, about not knowing whether or not her daughter was safe. She was concerned because she held a set of rational beliefs about threat-related uncertainty which had a number of effects that are characteristic of unworried concern. Here is an 'ABC' analysis of Veronica's concern.

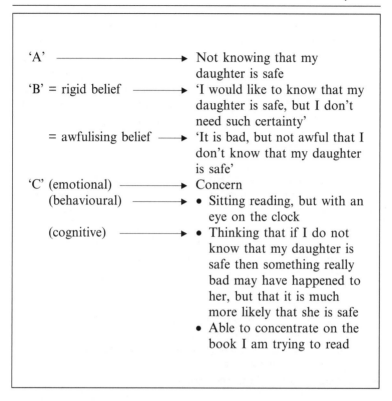

‘A’ —————————————→ Not knowing that my daughter is safe

‘B’ = rigid belief ————————→ ‘I would like to know that my daughter is safe, but I don’t need such certainty’

    = awfulising belief ——————→ ‘It is bad, but not awful that I don’t know that my daughter is safe’

‘C’ (emotional) —————————→ Concern

    (behavioural) ——————————→ • Sitting reading, but with an eye on the clock

    (cognitive) ————————————→ • Thinking that if I do not know that my daughter is safe then something really bad may have happened to her, but that it is much more likely that she is safe
                                           • Able to concentrate on the book I am trying to read

I hope you can see the differential effects that irrational and rational beliefs about threat-related uncertainty can have on a person’s feelings, behaviour and subsequent thinking.

How not to be afraid of flying

Intolerance of uncertainty is frequently at the root of so-called ‘fear of flying’. I actually dislike this term because the one thing that you are not afraid of is that the plane you are or will be travelling in will fly! You may think that the plane will crash or that you will lose control of yourself in some way due to feelings of anxiety, but you are not worried that the plane will fly. So let me concentrate on how you can fly without fear.

You can do so by holding a healthy philosophy about uncertainty. It is this:

'Many things are likely to happen on a plane which I am not going to understand and there will be much uncertainty. While it would be nice to understand what is going on, I really do not need to do so and I am going to assume that everything is fine until I get clear evidence to the contrary. On that point I have much evidence to support me concerning the safety of air travel, although I do recognise that plane crashes do happen and that I do not have immunity from being in one.'

In order to strengthen this attitude it is important that you act and think in ways that are consistent with it. This means that when, for example, you hear a noise that you don't understand, you don't do anything to find out what it is – for example, asking a flight attendant or the person in the next seat. While you won't be able to stop thoughts like 'Oh my God what was that', it is important that you *don't*:

- engage with the thoughts (e.g. by thinking about all the things that may have caused the noise)
- neutralise the thoughts (e.g. by reassuring yourself that there is nothing to worry about)
- distract yourself from the thoughts

Instead, the way to deal with such thoughts is to accept the fact that you have them and then get on with doing whatever it was you were doing before you had them while they are still in your mind. In this way, you will stop having such thoughts when you stop having such thoughts.

Before the flight, it is important that you do nothing to reassure yourself about the safety of air travel (e.g. by consulting the internet). Although, I mentioned that accepting the relative safety of flying is part of the healthy attitude that you need to take about uncertainty in this situation, the purpose of doing so is to acknowledge the reality (that it is very unlikely, but not impossible, that you may die in a plane crash, for example) rather than to reassure yourself that this threat does not exist.

If you follow the above advice you will not be afraid to fly. You still may not like doing so, but losing fear does not mean that enjoyment will follow.

Tolerating uncertainty and dealing with health-related concerns

If you want to deal healthily with threats to your well-being, then it is very important that you develop a healthy attitude towards not knowing if such threats as you may face are benign or serious. Here is how you can do this.

1   You identify a symptom or sign related to the possibility of ill health, in this case a spot on your arm that you have not noticed before. This sign or symptom is ambiguous. Thus, you are in a state of uncertainty with respect to your health.

2   You experience a sense of threat to your health. When you link this sense of threat to the sense of uncertainty mentioned above then you will experience health concern rather than health anxiety, but only when you hold a set of rational beliefs about this uncertainty-related threat to your health.

   This set of beliefs includes:

   (a) a flexible belief (e.g. 'I would like to know for sure right now that this spot on my arm is benign, but I don't need to have such certainty') and one or both of the following rational beliefs:

   (b) a non-awfulising belief (e.g. 'It is bad, but not awful if I don't know right now that this spot on my arm is benign')

   (c) a discomfort tolerance belief (e.g. 'It is difficult, but I can bear not knowing right now that this spot on my arm is benign')

3   Holding this set of rational beliefs about your uncertainty-related threat has three major effects:

   (a) It leads you to be concerned, but not anxious or worried, about your health, as we have seen.

   (b) You tend to think that if you don't know for sure that you are OK then this uncertainty means only that you are uncertain. You think that you are probably OK (e.g. 'If I do not know for sure that this spot is benign, then it is still probably benign'). However, you do not seek safety by attempting to reassure yourself in your mind that the spot is benign, as you lack the medical knowledge to do so.

   (c) It leads to behaviour that is designed to deal with the threat in a healthy manner. Thus, you consult your GP after a few weeks if the spot is still there, or sooner if it gets worse. You do not seek reassurance that the threat does not exist or avoid thinking about the existence of the threat. Thus, you do not do the following which are common responses in health anxiety, but not in health concern:

- You do not seek reassurance from others or from the internet that the threat does not exist. People who consult the internet about health issues often end up more rather than less convinced that there is something seriously wrong with them as such internet sites will feature remote possibilities of ill health.
- You do not check the spot frequently to see if it is getting better. If you do this, for example, by rubbing it, you will often make the spot worse.
- However, you do not refrain from looking at the spot altogether since you do need to check it once in a while to monitor its condition.

So what do you do instead? Once you have taken appropriate medical advice and resolved to follow it, you go about your business as you would if you did not have the spot.

Living in the 'uncertainty – probably well' quadrant

What do I mean by living in the 'uncertainty – probably well' quadrant? To answer this question, I need to explain the four quadrants that are relevant here.

	Well	Ill
Certainty	1	2
Uncertainty	3	4

Quadrant 1: 'certainty – well'

Here you seek medical advice and you are told that your spot is benign. As you hold a set of rational beliefs, you believe this and you don't seek any further form of treatment beyond what you have sought already. Being concerned about your health, however, you ask your GP for a reasonable time-frame concerning the disappearance of the spot and what you should do if it gets worse. You only seek further treatment on the basis of this advice.

Quadrant 2: 'certainty – ill'

Here you know for sure that your spot is malignant. You act on the medical advice you are given, and seek appropriate treatment, but because your beliefs are rational rather than irrational you do not think that your condition is worse than you have been told.

Quadrant 3: 'uncertainty – probably well'

In this quadrant, you are in a state of uncertainty, but the evidence indicates that you are probably well. There is no clear evidence that you are ill and you are much more likely, most of the time, to be in this quadrant than you are to be in quadrant 4 (below). So, you have been told that your spot is probably benign, but there is an outside chance that it could be malignant. Holding a set of rational, rather than irrational, beliefs about uncertainty, you conclude that your spot is probably benign and go about your business on this basis, but you seek and follow guidance concerning signs of malignancy.

Quadrant 4: 'uncertainty – probably ill'

Here you are in a state of uncertainty, but the reality is that you are probably ill. Thus, your doctor says that your spot is probably malignant. Here it is sensible to take steps to address the problem because the signs point to you being ill. If you held irrational beliefs about uncertainty you would assume that the spot was definitely malignant, but as your beliefs are rational, you proceed on the basis that you are ill, but do not rule out that you may not be.

The main issue here is that your rational beliefs about uncertainty with respect to a threat to your heath will enable you to process and act on the odds that are either in your favour or against you. They do not lead you to overestimate or defensively underestimate the risks you are facing as would be the case if your beliefs were irrational.

General guidance about how to deal with uncertainty-based problems

If you have problems with uncertainty, let me end this chapter by giving you some general advice about dealing with them.

1 State what your problem with uncertainty is

This involves you doing the following:

(a) Specify the situational contexts in which the problem occurs.
(b) Indicate what you are most disturbed about in these situations (this is the 'A' in the ABC framework).
(c) List the major unhealthy negative emotion that you experience about 'A' (this is the emotional 'C' in the ABC framework).
(d) List how you act or feel like acting when you experience your emotional 'C' (this is the behavioural 'C' in the ABC framework).
(e) List how you think when you experience your emotional 'C' (this is known as the thinking or cognitive 'C').
(f) Identify your rigid belief and your main extreme belief about 'A' that explains your emotional, behavioural and thinking responses at 'C' (these beliefs occur at 'B' in the ABC framework).

2 State your healthy goals in dealing with such uncertainty

This involves you doing the following:

(a) Specify the situational contexts in which the problem occurs (this will be the same as in 1(a) above).
(b) Indicate what you are most disturbed about in these situations (this is the 'A' in the ABC framework and will again be the same as in 1(b) above).
(c) List the major negative emotion that it would be healthy for you to experience about 'A'. This is your emotional goal.
(d) List your constructive alternative behaviours and action tendencies. This is your behavioural goal.
(e) List the more realistic thinking that would accompany your new healthy negative emotion. This is your thinking goal.
(f) Identify your flexible belief and your main non-extreme belief about 'A' that underpin your emotional, behavioural and thinking goals at 'C'.

3 Develop reasons why your rational beliefs are rational and your irrational beliefs are irrational

This involves you doing the following:

(a) Develop reasons why your rational (i.e. flexible and non-extreme) beliefs are:
  - True
  - Logical
  - Productive.
(b) Develop reasons why your irrational (i.e. rigid and extreme) beliefs are:
  - False
  - Illogical
  - Unproductive.

4 Act and think in ways that are consistent with your rational belief and inconsistent with your irrational belief

This involves you doing the following:

- Go about your business, living with uncertainty while rehearsing your rational beliefs about uncertainty. This means refraining from doing anything that is designed to rid yourself of doubt and uncertainty. Only take action that a person who has a healthy set of beliefs about uncertainty would take. If in doubt about this, do nothing.

5 Let the irrational 'voices' be

Realise that when you don't act to eradicate doubt then the part of your mind that is operating according to your set of irrational beliefs will come more to the fore. Rather than respond to each of these highly distorted thoughts, recognise where they are coming from and regard them as you would voices on the radio that you are aware of but choose not to listen to. Also do not try not to think these thoughts. When you do practise thinking realistically to strengthen your set of rational beliefs do so only once per episode. To do so more often is to fall prey to using such thoughts as an inappropriate source of self-reassurance, which will only maintain your problem and not deal with it effectively.

The case of Maggie

Here is how Maggie (whom we met at the beginning of the chapter) used the above schema to help her deal with her uncertainty-related problem. When reading what follows refer back to the schema presented above where necessary.

My problem with uncertainty

- The situational contexts in which my problem occurs: *Whenever my daughter is late.*
- 'A' (what I am most disturbed about): *Not knowing that my daughter is safe.*
- *Emotional 'C': Anxiety.*
  Behavioural 'C': I keep ringing her mobile to see where she is and I ring her friends if I don't get any reply.
  Thinking 'C': I imagine all kinds of negative things happening to her.
- Irrational beliefs ('B'):
  Rigid belief: *I must know that my daughter is safe.*
  Awfulising belief: *It's terrible not to know that she is safe.*

My healthy goals in dealing with such uncertainty

- The situational contexts in which my problem occurs: *Whenever my daughter is late.*
- 'A' (what I want to deal with more effectively): *Not knowing that my daughter is safe.*
- *My emotional goal* (the major negative emotion that it would be healthy for me to experience about 'A'): *Concern* (rather than anxiety).
  My behavioural goal (my constructive alternative behaviours and action tendencies): *Get on with whatever I am doing* (rather than keep ringing her mobile to see where she is and rather than ringing her friends).
  My subsequent thinking goal (the more realistic thinking that accompanies my new healthy negative emotion): *Thinking that she is probably safe and acknowledging that despite doing so I will still think in a distorted way. But I will get on with things while not engaging with or trying to distract myself from such thoughts.*
- My flexible belief and main non-extreme belief about 'A' that underpin my emotional, behavioural and thinking goals at 'C'.

Flexible belief: *I really want to know that my daughter is safe, but I don't have to have such certainty.*
Non-awfulising belief: *It's bad not to know that she is safe, but it is not the end of the world.*

Reasons why my rational beliefs are rational and my irrational beliefs are irrational

It is true that I want to know for sure that my daughter is safe. This is my desire and I cannot pretend otherwise. Sadly, it is also true that I don't have to have the certainty that I want. If there were a law that I had to have this guarantee, then I would have it, which clearly I don't, so my demand that I have to know that my daughter is safe is clearly false. Also it is clearly illogical for me to think that because I want such certainty it must exist. My desire does not have any effect on what exists. But, it is logical for me to note that I don't have to have what I want. This clearly makes sense. Finally, my flexible belief yields much healthier results for me than my rigid belief.

When comparing my non-extreme non-awfulising belief with my extreme awfulising belief, the first is clearly true, while the second is false. I can prove that it is bad if I do not know if my daughter is safe and also that it is not the end of the world if I don't have such certainty. If it were the end of the world, then nothing could be worse than not having such certainty. If this were true, then it would be very strange since it would mean that such uncertainty would be worse than the death of my daughter, which is clearly ridiculous. Also, my non-extreme belief makes sense whereas my extreme belief does not. For when I jump from saying that it is bad not to know that my daughter is safe to saying that it is the end of the world, I am making an illogical leap in saying that something extreme follows logically from something non-extreme. Well, it doesn't. Whereas in my non-extreme belief, the second non-extreme component (i.e. 'it is not the end of the world not having the certainty that my daughter is safe') follows logically from the first non-extreme component (i.e. 'it is bad not knowing that my daughter is safe'). Finally, my non-extreme non-awfulising belief also yields better results for me (emotionally, behaviourally and cognitively) than does my extreme awfulising belief.

Actions and thoughts that are consistent with my rational belief and inconsistent with my irrational belief

When my daughter is late and I don't know that she is safe, I am going to trust her to call me if she needs to. While I will still feel the urge to call her, I am not going to act on this urge. Instead I am going to get on with whatever I would be getting on with if I knew she was safe. I will briefly remind myself that uncertainty is not inherently dangerous and that she is probably safe. I am not going to do this more than once though. Otherwise I would be using this sensible thought as an unhealthy self-reassurance strategy. I still expect to have distorted thoughts about her safety. After all, I have been having such thoughts for years, but I am not going to engage with them or try to banish them from my mind. I am going to treat them as lingering reverberations from my irrational beliefs and get on with whatever activity I am involved with.

A realistic rational tolerance of uncertainty credo

In this final section, I will outline what I call a realistic rational tolerance of uncertainty credo. This is comprised of a set of beliefs which promote healthy responses to uncertainty. I will again put this credo in the first person and as you read it bear in mind that it is a general credo which needs to be applied to specific instances of uncertainty.

As a human being I recognise that I do not like uncertainty, particularly when I am facing some kind of threat, and I prefer to know at all times that I am safe. However, when my preference in this respect is strong, I tend to demand that I must have certainty that I am safe from threat. It is a real struggle for me to acknowledge that no matter how strong my desire is for certainty, sadly and regretfully, this does not mean that I have to have my desire met. In the journey towards believing this, I may well do many things to deal with my disturbed feelings which may help me in the short term, but not in the long term. Thus, I may deny that the threat exists or I may seek reassurance that it does not exist. However, I recognise that trying to get certainty by these means when I am facing uncertainty is not healthy and I can use such attempts as cues to think rationally about uncertainty as soon as I am able. While I see that I can do this, I also acknowledge that there will be times when I won't. The path towards dealing healthily with uncertainty is a rocky one. When I do eventually think rationally about uncertainty, I will accept that when I don't get my desire met in this respect, I will feel badly about this, even though I have acknowledged that I don't have to get what I want. These bad feelings are healthy. They are a sign that I have a desire for certainty, that this desire is not being met and they motivate me to change things if they can be changed and to adjust constructively if they can't be changed. However, I also recognise that it is very difficult for me to have a desire for certainty and to keep this desire flexible in the face of uncertainty. As such, I will return to disturbed negative feelings when I go back to holding a rigid demand.

I also recognise that when my desire for certainty that I am safe is not met, and I face such uncertainty, I tend to think that it is awful and the end of the world when this happens, particularly when I transform my desire for certainty into a rigid demand for certainty. When I do so, I cannot see any possibility that I am safe, although I desperately seek such reassurance.

It is a real struggle for me to accept that when my desire for certainty is not met, this is bad and unfortunate but not terrible or the end of the world. I can believe this, but I will oscillate between thinking in this way and thinking that it is awful until I make the former stronger than the latter. This will be interspersed with attempts to reassure myself. When I do eventually operate according to my non-awfulising belief, I will be in a better frame of mind to acknowledge that I can be safe even though I do not have certainty.

I also recognise that when I face uncertainty in the context of a possible threat and my desire for certainty is thus not met, I tend to think that it is unbearable when this happens and that the threat is bound to materialise. I do this particularly when I transform my desire for certainty into a rigid demand. It is again a real struggle for me to accept that when my desire for certainty is not met, this is bearable and that I can bear it. I realise that I can believe this, but I will oscillate between believing that I can bear it and believing that I can't until I make the former stronger than the latter. This will again be interspersed with attempts to reassure myself that I am safe in order to quickly get rid of my disturbed feelings. When I do believe that I can bear uncertainty, I am in a better frame of mind to see how much of a threat I am really facing.

In the face of uncertainty, I tend to depreciate the whole of life and really struggle to accept that life is a complex mixture of the good, the bad and the neutral. When I do attain such acceptance, with the usual oscillations between life-acceptance, life-depreciation and seeking reassurance in the face of threat-related uncertainty, which may not be until a considerable amount of time has passed, then I will see that the existence of uncertainty does not change the complexity of life. The complexity of life incorporates uncertainty and certainty as well as many neutral events.

While flexible and non-extreme beliefs will help me to develop tolerance of uncertainty, I recognise that even when I work hard to develop such beliefs, I will often return to thinking rigidly and in extreme ways. Similarly, I acknowledge that as I work to internalise this realistic credo, I will experience many lapses along the way. The best way of dealing with these lapses is to accept them, without liking them, learn specific things from them and act on such specific learning in relevant future situations.

When I do disturb myself about uncertainty, I will struggle with that and may well disturb myself for thus disturbing myself. I will strive to accept myself for disturbing myself about uncertainty and I recognise that as I do so my efforts will oscillate between accepting myself and depreciating myself and various forms of denial. If I persevere, my self-acceptance will gain ascendancy and, as it does so, I will also acknowledge that while it is desirable that I do not disturb myself, I am not immune from doing so. However, I will struggle with this too and at times will go back to demanding that I must not disturb myself about uncertainty. Once I have largely accepted myself for disturbing myself, I can then go back and work on the original disturbance.

So what are the advantages and disadvantages of a realistic rational tolerance of uncertainty credo? I first discussed the advantages and disadvantages of holding such a credo in Chapter 2. Applying these to the realistic rational tolerance of uncertainty credo presented above, we may say the following.

The advantages of this credo seem to be:

1 It gives people a warts-and-all picture of rational uncertainty tolerance that is within the grasp of most people.
2 Even though periods of irrational thinking and reassurance-seeking are present in realistic rational uncertainty tolerance, there is still a clear indication of the rational thinking that people should aim for.
3 It can comfort rather than inspire and can thus motivate those people who value realism in their quest for greater tolerance of uncertainty.

However, there are disadvantages to the realistic rational tolerance of uncertainty credo. These are:

1 It may legitimise disturbance and reassurance-seeking as necessary components of tolerance of uncertainty, whereas, in reality, they are frequently rather than inevitably occurring components.
2 It may discourage those people who are capable of a more ideal form of tolerance of uncertainty (i.e. one relatively free from disturbance and reassurance-seeking).

Tolerance of uncertainty is often linked to self-control and I will discuss this issue in the next and final chapter.

Chapter 10

Self-control

Introduction

If it is a truism to say that we live in an uncertain world, it is also a truism to say that we are not in control of the universe. We have some control over what happens, but not as much as we would like. Given this, we need to develop and maintain a healthy set of beliefs, particularly when we lack control over our lives and even over ourselves. Paradoxically, as I will show you later, adopting a healthy attitude towards lacking control is a powerful way of gaining a sense of control.

Some of you may be familiar with the serenity prayer, which I have modified slightly to fit our subject of control:

> God grant me courage to control what I can control, serenity to accept what I can't control and wisdom to know the difference.

Bear this prayer in mind as you read this chapter as I will be referring to its component parts.

What is control?

Control refers to a situation where you can, or 'feel' you can, bring about a direct outcome or exert some influence over something.

When you are, or 'feel' that you are, 'in control', this often refers to a situation where either (a) your attempts to effect a positive outcome or to prevent a negative outcome are successful, or (b) you 'feel' that these attempts will be successful.

When you are not in control, this tends to refer to the opposite of the above, i.e. a situation where either (a) your attempts to effect a positive outcome or to prevent a negative outcome are not successful, or (b) you 'feel' that these attempts will not be successful. How you respond to not being in control is a marker of psychological health or psychological disturbance.

Control: external vs. internal

It is very important to distinguish between what I call here internal control and external control. When you have or 'feel' that you have internal control, you are able to exert direct control (or 'feel' that you can) over those things internal to you. (i.e. your behaviours, thoughts and images, feelings and controllable aspects of your bodily and physical functioning).

When you have or 'feel' that you have external control, you are able to exert some influence (or 'feel' that you can) over those things external to you (i.e. other people and aspects of your environment).

This analysis shows that, as a general rule, you have *direct control* (potentially at any rate, as I will discuss presently) over yourself and that you have *influence*, but not direct control, over others, and that the situation is mixed with respect to aspects of your environment.

External control: developing healthy responses

In this section, I am going to discuss developing the courage to exert control over what you can control or influence and developing serenity to accept what you can't control externally.

Developing courage to exert external control

When you have courage to exert control over people and things external to you, you are basically in a concerned, rather than an anxious state and you take action despite feeling concerned. Courage is not the absence of feelings of concern. It is characterised by taking action when concerned.

In the ABC framework, the emotional 'C' in this case is concern and the behavioural 'C' is taking action in order to exert external control. 'A' is some kind of threat and 'B' is the flexible and non-extreme beliefs that the person holds about the threat at 'A' that account for his concern and action at 'C'.

Common threats at 'A' in this regard centre on a prediction that exerted control will have a negative impact for the person (e.g. disapproval, friction between people, demotion at work, being criticised, or uncertainty about the possible outcome of such exerted control).

Let me exemplify this by considering a common situation where a person develops a sense of being in control at work as a result of asserting herself with a co-worker. Fiona works in a health club and her colleague, Holly, tries to get her to do all the things that she, Holly, does not like doing. Fiona does not agree to do this and, as a result, feels in control of what happens to her at work. She asserts herself and says 'no' to Holly consistently with the result that Holly eventually gets the message and stops asking her to do unpleasant things for her. Fiona asserts herself despite thinking that if she takes such action there could be an unpleasant atmosphere at work between her and Holly. Let me outline Fiona's ABC.

1. Fiona's 'C'
    I am concerned.
2. Fiona's 'A'
    There will be a bad atmosphere between me and Holly if I assert myself with her.
3. Fiona's rational beliefs at 'B'
    I would like things to be harmonious between Holly and me, but it doesn't have to be the way I want it to be. It is difficult, but I can bear it if there is an atmosphere between us and it is worth it to me to do so because I need to assert boundaries between Holly and me.

Developing the serenity to accept what you can't control in the external world

As every assertiveness trainer will tell you, assertiveness increases your chances of getting a positive outcome, but does not guarantee you achieving that outcome. As such, it is important that you develop the serenity to accept it when you cannot bring about your desired outcome in the external world.

Let's suppose that Fiona asserted herself with her colleague, Holly, but to no avail. Holly kept on trying to get Fiona to do her dirty work for her and although Fiona was steadfast in her refusal, Holly kept trying. How can Fiona accept the fact that she cannot successfully exert external control over Holly, meaning that Holly is impervious to Fiona's assertive attempts to influence her? This is how.

Step 1: Fiona recognises that her attempts to influence Holly have not worked.

Step 2: Fiona develops a set of rational, acceptance-based beliefs about her lack of control in this area. These beliefs are as follows:

- 'I would like Holly to stop trying to palm off her unpleasant work on me, but she does not have to do this. She is a free agent and can choose to ignore my assertive attempts to get her to stop.'
- 'It is bad that I cannot get Holly to stop trying to palm off her work on to me, but it isn't the end of the world if she keeps doing so.'
- 'It is a struggle for me to put up with not being able to get Holly to stop trying to palm off her unpleasant tasks on to me, but I can tolerate this and it is worth it to me to do so since it will help me to stay in employment until I am able to get a better job.'
- 'While this aspect of life is bad, the whole of life is not bad. It is a complex mixture of positive, negative (including this one) and neutral aspects.'

Step 3: Fiona gets on with her life while acting and thinking in ways consistent with her rational beliefs.

Having developed her set of acceptance-based rational beliefs about her lack of external control or, more strictly speaking, influence over Holly's behaviour, Fiona continues with her life at work and at home. She does not dwell on her lack of external control. Rather, Fiona reminds herself that while she cannot influence Holly to stop her behaviour, she still has internal control in the sense that she can say 'no' to Holly every time she tries to get Fiona to do mundane tasks for her.

This last point is very important. It is really the essence of the serenity part of the serenity prayer. For when you adopt a set of rational beliefs about what you cannot control in the external world, you are developing a powerful sense of what you can control in the internal world. This is the value of acceptance. It may not give you serenity, but you do not disturb yourself about your lack of external control and therefore you can move on with your life.

Internal control: developing healthy responses

When you experience problems with internal control, you are unable (or 'feel' you are unable) to control one of your internal processes such as your behaviour, your thinking or your feelings. There are two healthy responses to this. First, you need to deal with such loss of control in a non-disturbed manner. Second, you may need to use a counter-intuitive, but effective way of bringing about internal control.

Dealing healthily with losing internal control

Here is how you can remain undisturbed when you begin to lose control of your behaviour, your thinking and your emotions. Let me deal with these one at a time.

Responding healthily to losing behavioural control

I made the point in Chapter 1 when considering behaviour that there is a distinction between an urge to act (or what is often called an action tendency) and overt behaviour. Thus, you may feel the urge to punch someone in the face, but normally you will not act on that urge. Thus, a person can think that they are losing control when they act in a certain way, but also when they experience having an action tendency as evidence that they are losing control.

Here is an example of how not to disturb yourself about losing behavioural control. Suzanne was shopping in an up-market department store in London for her husband's birthday. After she had bought what she was looking for she decided to browse in the store for a while. Whilst browsing, Suzanne saw a handbag that she had always wanted, but which was well out of her price range. Suddenly, Suzanne felt a very strong urge to steal the handbag. However, she did not disturb herself about this urge. She reacted to this with concern, but went about her business. Subsequently, she did not avoid the store as she might have done if she had disturbed herself about having the urge. Using the ABC framework let's see if we can understand Suzanne's reaction.

'A' = *I experienced a strong urge to steal a handbag in the store which is evidence that I was losing control of myself.*

'B' = *I don't like the fact that I was losing control of myself, but that does not mean that I must not do so. It is bad, but not awful that I was doing so.*

'C' (emotional)   = *Concern.*

(behavioural) = *Staying in the store and going back whenever I need to.*

(thinking)   = *Having an urge to steal the handbag does not mean that I will steal it.*
I have control over such urges.

Please note one very important point. Suzanne's rational belief about her loss of self-control (as she construed her urge to steal the handbag) led not only to a healthy emotional reaction and constructive behavioural reaction at 'C', but also to a realistic thinking response at 'C'. I discussed the thinking consequences of irrational and rational beliefs on p. 16 in Chapter 2 and I refer you to that section for full coverage of this point.

In Suzanne's case, her rational belief led her to conclude that if she had stayed in the store the experience of the urge would not have inevitably led her to steal the handbag. She concluded, therefore, that she had control when she experienced this urge.

Responding healthily to losing control of one's thinking

I have alluded to how to deal with losing thinking control when discussing Suzanne's case above, but let me now do so more thoroughly. One of the design features of being human, in my view, is that we do not have perfect control over the way we think. People who meditate, even those who are expert at it, will tell you that when they focus on their particular mantra, all kinds of thoughts come into their mind which take them away from their focus. Part of meditation therefore is to understand that non-mantra thoughts will come into one's mind and what is important is the stance that one takes to these irrelevant thoughts. This healthy stance involves you accepting the existence of these thoughts and letting them be without engaging with them or attempting to banish them. This is the stance that people who practise meditation a lot learn to implement and I will return to this issue later.

When you have a thought, a way of thinking or mental images that indicate to you that you are beginning to lose control of your thinking and you remain undisturbed about it then you do so because you hold a set of rational beliefs about your thinking.

Here is an example. Ruth went to visit Delia, her best friend, who had just had a baby. They were talking in Delia's kitchen and Ruth was cutting up an onion with a knife when she had the thought 'What would it be like to stab Delia's baby'. There was no urge attached to the thought (unlike with Suzanne above). Ruth's concern was that her alien thought meant that she was losing control of her thinking. The following ABC explains how Ruth remained undisturbed about this.

A = *I thought what it would be like to stab Delia's baby. This is an alien thought that means I am beginning to lose control of my thinking.*

B = *I prefer to be in complete control of my thinking, but I do not have to be so. Having alien thoughts that I can't control is unpleasant and unwanted, but not terrible.*

C (emotional) = *Concern.*

   (behavioural) = *Going to see Delia and her baby.*
                                  Approaching other babies.
                                  Holding sharp knives.

   (thinking) = *Having such thoughts is in all probability evidence of the paradoxical nature of my mind and not evidence that I will harm Delia's baby and other babies.*
                                  I will have a baby if I want to have one. I have no evidence that I will harm it.

Responding healthily to losing emotional control

Your beliefs about your emotions determine how much in control you 'feel' when you experience them. While you may put a rein on positive emotions because you are concerned about losing control if you feel them, it is more the negative emotions you are concerned about because of the risk of losing internal control.

In particular, you are more likely to 'feel' that you are losing internal control when you experience anger and anxiety. Here is how to deal healthily with both of these emotions.

• **Anger**

If you are concerned, but not anxious about experiencing anger because you think you will lose internal control as a result, then you hold a rational belief about this feeling. You may believe that while you would prefer not to feel anger, there is no reason why you must not feel this emotion and if you did it would be bad, but not terrible. As a result you do not avoid confrontations where you are likely to feel anger and you will assert yourself when you need to.

• **Anxiety**

Many people fear anxiety and because they believe that they must gain control of this emotion immediately, they become more anxious rather than less. Here is how to respond healthily to this loss of control.

First, as elsewhere, be flexible and not rigid about experiencing anxiety. If you believe that you would rather not be anxious, but you don't have to get rid of this feeling, and if you prove to yourself that anxiety is a painful, but bearable emotion, then you will begin the process of developing a sense of internal control in response to being anxious.

Second, show yourself that experiencing anxiety is unfortunate, but hardly the end of the world. It is a painful emotion to be sure, but not an unbearable one, and if you see that it is worth bearing (since bearing anxiety allows you to deal constructively with threat rather than avoid it), then these attitudes will also help you to restore a sense of control in the face of anxiety.

Western, Eastern and Paradoxical approaches to losing internal control

Developing and practising rational beliefs about losing internal control is perhaps the most important thing you can do to regain a greater sense of internal control. While there are a number of strategies designed to promote such control, none of them will help you in the longer term unless you have these rational beliefs in place.

I distinguish between Western, Eastern and Paradoxical approaches to regaining internal control. The Western approach to regaining internal control is based on the idea that you need to do something in order to regain internal control. Once you have done this and it works, you will have regained a sense of internal control.

By contrast, the Eastern approach is based on the idea of not doing anything when you feel out of control. Rather, you acknowledge and accept whatever it is that you are experiencing. While the Western approach is explicit in stating that the application of certain techniques is designed to yield a greater sense of internal control, with the Eastern approach this design is more implicit. Otherwise, what is the point of adopting a 'do nothing, acceptance-based' approach if it is not designed to bring about the same result as the Western approach?

Finally, the Paradoxical approach to gaining internal control is counter-intuitive. It involves you doing the reverse of what your common sense tells you to do. Thus, if you have an intrusive, unwanted thought, your common sense tells you to get rid of it. By contrast, the Paradoxical approach encourages you to repeat the thought many times until you get used to it or bored with it and it therefore loses its disturbing sting, as it were.

The Eastern approach to gaining internal control

Let's consider the Eastern approach to gaining internal control.

- **Thinking**

A well-known psychology experiment showed that when you ask people to think about a white bear and then instruct them not to think about it then these people report that this instruction does not work (Wegner, 1994). Trying not to think something is not an effective strategy, plain and simple.

So if you have a thought that is alien to you, an intrusive thought that you would rather not have, then trying not to have this thought just won't work. Instead, a better strategy, based on the Eastern approach, is to acknowledge the existence of the thought, and that is it! Here, it is important not to engage with the thought (for example, to reassure yourself that the thought is not dangerous), to eradicate the thought or to distract yourself from the thought. Once you have acknowledged the existence of the thought, then it is important that you get on with whatever you would have been doing if you had not had the thought. If you do this you will become aware eventually that you are not thinking the thought. This awareness will bring the thought back into your mind. The best way of responding to this is to do what you did before: accept the thought and then get on with life.

- **Emotions**

The Eastern approach to emotions is again to acknowledge that you are feeling a certain way and then to do nothing to get rid of this feeling or to engage with it. This approach is based on the idea that all emotions, whether they are healthy or unhealthy, are part of the human experience and it is not the feelings themselves that pose a problem for you. Rather, it is how you tend to respond to these feelings. In particular, your attempts to stop the experience are regarded, within the Eastern approach, as particularly problematic.

- **Behaviour**

As I pointed out in Chapter 1, when we consider behaviour we need to distinguish between overt behaviour and action tendencies (or urges to act). The Eastern approach to behaviour is as follows.

- **Overt behaviour**. The Eastern approach to behaviour recommends that when you have acted in a way that is unconstructive, your response is to acknowledge and accept that you acted in this way. This stance is intended to prevent you from disturbing yourself about the way you acted and will help you to reflect on the reasons why you acted in the way that you did. My own view is that you will be best placed to do this if your beliefs about your behaviour are rational.
- **Action tendencies**. The Eastern approach to action tendencies is again to acknowledge and to accept that you have such urges and therefore you neither have to act on them nor to eradicate them. Again it is good advice as long as your beliefs about these urges are rational.

The Western approach to gaining internal control

The Western approach is based on the idea that when you experience a disturbed emotion or an unconstructive behaviour or action tendency, you can deal with these responses as follows. First you need to assess what you are most disturbed about and then identify the irrational beliefs that underpin your disturbed response. You can help yourself by challenging these beliefs and developing rational alternatives to these beliefs. Then, you need to act on these rational beliefs and accept that your disturbed feelings, distorted thoughts and urges to act in unconstructive ways will not change until you have implemented your rational beliefs and have acted in ways that strengthen them over time. How long does this process take? It takes as long as it takes until your beliefs are rational and impact constructively on your feelings, behaviour and subsequent thinking. When you have achieved this you will have gained an enduring sense of internal control.

The Paradoxical approach to gaining internal control

As I alluded to above, the Paradoxical approach to gaining internal control urges you to repeat something until you get bored with it and it loses its disturbability. For example, Harold had the thought that he might stab his girlfriend while they were watching TV. Using the Paradoxical approach to gaining internal control, he passed a sharp knife across his girlfriend's neck (with her informed consent) many times until he got bored with it.

Debra, a religious woman who thought about having sex with Jesus and avoided all things religious, helped herself to gain a sense of control over her thoughts, by repeating to herself many times 'I want to have sex with Jesus'. She did so until she became thoroughly bored with this thought and thus gained a sense of internal control over her thinking.

Having outlined these three approaches to gaining internal control, I invite you to use the approach which you think will help you the most. Use it and evaluate its results. If it works for you, use it. If not, experiment with one or both of the other approaches.

My own opinion on this issue is that if you are disturbing yourself about not having as much external or internal control as you would like, you deal with the underlying irrational beliefs as outlined in the

Western approach to gaining control. Then, use the Eastern or the Paradoxical approach until you feel in greater control of yourself and the controllable aspects of the world around you.

Realistic rational self-control credo

In this final section, I will outline what I call a realistic rational self-control credo. This is comprised of a set of beliefs which promote healthy responses to situations where you may be beginning to lose control. I will again put this credo in the first person and as you read it bear in mind that it is a general credo which needs to be applied to specific instances of threats to self-control.

As a human being I recognise that I do not like losing self-control. However, when my preference in this respect is strong, I tend to demand that I must not lose self-control. It is a real struggle for me to acknowledge that no matter how strong my desire is for self-control, sadly and regretfully, this does not mean that I have to have my desire met. In the journey towards believing this, I may well do many things to deal with my disturbed feelings which may help me in the short term, but not in the long term. Thus, I may well try to regain immediate self-control or I may over-compensate for the threat. However, I recognise that trying to get self-control by these means is not healthy and I can use them as cues to think rationally about losing self-control as soon as I am able. While I recognise that I can do this, I also acknowledge that there will be times when I won't. The path towards dealing healthily with threats to self-control is a rocky one. When I do eventually think rationally about such threats, I will accept that when I don't get my desire met in this respect, I will feel badly about this, even though I have accepted that I don't have to get what I want. These bad feelings are healthy. They are a sign that I have desires for self-control, that these desires are not being met and they motivate me to control myself if I can and to accept it if I can't. However, I also recognise that it is very difficult for me to have desires about self-control and to keep these desires flexible in the face of losing such control. As such I will return to disturbed negative feelings when I go back to holding rigid demands.

I also recognise that when my desire for self-control is not met and I face a threat to such control, I tend to think that it is awful and the end of the world when this happens, and especially when I transform my desire for self-control into a need for such control. When I do so, I cannot see any possibility that I can regain self-control. It is a real struggle for me to accept that when my desire for self-control is not met, this is bad and unfortunate but not terrible or the end of the world. I can believe this, but I will oscillate between thinking in this way and thinking that it is awful until I make the former stronger than the latter. This will be interspersed with attempts to regain immediate self-control or to over-compensate for losing self-control. When I do eventually operate according to my non-awfulising belief, I will be in a better frame of mind to acknowledge that I can gain self-control even though I am losing it.

I also recognise that when I face a threat to self-control and my desire for self-control is thus not met, I tend to think that it is unbearable when this happens, and that the threat is bound to materialise when I transform this desire into a demand. It is again a real struggle for me to accept that when my desire for self-control is not met, this is bearable and that I can bear it. I realise that I can believe this, but I will oscillate between believing that I can bear it and believing that I can't until I make the former stronger than the latter. This will again be interspersed with attempts to gain immediate self-control or to over-compensate for this in order to quickly get rid of my disturbed feelings. When I do believe that I can bear losing self-control, I am in a better frame of mind to see how much of a threat to my self-control I am really facing.

In the face of losing self-control, I may tend to depreciate myself and, when I do, I find it a real struggle to acknowledge that I am a fallible human being equal in worth to all other human beings although we differ in a myriad of different respects. I can eventually do this, but recognise that I will oscillate between depreciating myself and accepting myself interspersed with making attempts to regain immediate self-control or to over-compensate for losing self-control until I make my self-acceptance belief stronger than my self-depreciation belief. When I do this I can see that this belief will help me to stand back and learn how best to regain self-control when I am losing it. I will work steadily to do this and, in striving to do so, I realise that I will often go back to depreciating myself and even when I basically accept myself I will occasionally depreciate myself.

Also, in the face of a threat to my self-control, I may tend to depreciate the whole of life and really struggle to accept that life is a complex mixture of the good, the bad and the neutral. When I do attain such acceptance, with the usual oscillations between life-acceptance, life-depreciation, trying to gain immediate self-control in the face of losing self-control and over-compensating for this, which may not be until a considerable amount of time has passed, then, I will see that the existence of a threat to self-control does not change the complexity of life. The complexity of life incorporates having self-control and losing such controls as well as many neutral events.

While flexible and non-extreme beliefs will help me to respond healthily to losing self-control, I recognise that even when I work hard to develop such beliefs, I will often return to thinking rigidly and in extreme ways. Similarly, I acknowledge that as I work to internalise this realistic credo, I will experience many lapses along the way. The best way of dealing with these lapses is to accept them, without liking them, learn specific things from them and act on such specific learning in relevant future situations.

When I do disturb myself about losing self-control, I will struggle with that and may well disturb myself for thus disturbing myself. I will strive to accept myself for disturbing myself about losing self-control and I recognise that as I do so my efforts will oscillate between accepting myself and depreciating myself and various forms of trying to gain immediate self-control. If I persevere, I will help my self-acceptance to gain ascendancy and, as this happens, I will acknowledge that while it is desirable that I do not disturb myself, I am not immune from doing so, and nor do I have to be immune. However, I will struggle with this too and at times will go back to demanding that I must not disturb myself about losing self-control. Once I have largely accepted myself for disturbing myself, I can then go back and work on the original disturbance.

So what are the advantages and disadvantages of a realistic rational self-control credo? I first discussed the advantages and disadvantages of holding such a credo in Chapter 2. Applying these to the realistic rational self-control credo presented above, we may say the following.

The advantages of this credo seem to be:

1 It gives people a warts-and-all picture of rational self-control that is within the grasp of most people.
2 Even though periods of irrational thinking and making attempts to gain immediate self-control are present in realistic rational self-control, there is still a clear indication of the rational thinking that people should aim for.
3 It can comfort rather than inspire and can thus motivate those people who value realism in their quest for greater self-control.

However, there are disadvantages to the realistic rational self-control credo. These are:

1 It may legitimise disturbance and attempts to gain immediate self-control as necessary components of self-control, whereas, in reality, they are frequently rather than inevitably occurring components.
2 It may discourage those people who are capable of a more ideal form of self-control (i.e. one relatively free from disturbance and attempts to regain immediate self-control).

We have now reached the end of the book. I hope that you have found it constructive and would welcome any feedback (c/o the publisher).

References

De Bono, E. (1991). *I Am Right, You Are Wrong*. London: Penguin Books.

Dryden, W. (2009a). *Understanding Emotional Problems: The REBT Perspective*. Hove, East Sussex: Routledge.

Dryden, W. (2009b). *Rational Emotive Behaviour Therapy: Distinctive Features*. London: Routledge.

Dryden, W. (2009c). *Self-discipline: How to Get it and How to Keep it*. London: Sheldon.

Dryden, W. and Branch, R. (2008). *The Fundamentals of Rational Emotive Behaviour Therapy: A Training Handbook*. 2nd edn. Chichester: Wiley.

Ellenberger, H.F. (1970). *The Discovery of the Unconscious: The History and Evolution of Dynamic Psychiatry*. New York: Basic Books.

Ellis, A. (1976). The biological basis of human irrationality. *Journal of Individual Psychology*, 32, 145–168.

Ellis, A. (1994). *Reason and Emotion in Psychotherapy*. Revised and updated edn. New York: Birch Lane Press.

Flach, F. (1997). *How to Bounce Back When the Going Gets Tough*. New York: Hatherleigh Press.

Hayes, S.C. and Strosahl, K.D. (eds) (2004). *A Practical Guide to Acceptance and Commitment Therapy*. New York: Springer-Verlag.

Maslow, A. (1968). *Toward a Psychology of Being*. New York: Van Nostrand Reinhold.

Wahba, A. and Bridgewell, L. (1976). Maslow reconsidered: a review of research on the need hierarchy theory. *Organizational Behavior and Human Performance*, 15, 212–240.

Wegner, D. (1994). *White Bears and Other Unwanted Thoughts: Suppression, Obsession, and the Psychology of Mental Control*. New York: Guilford Press.

Index

ABC framework 118–19, 127–32; behavioural control 163; external control 159–60; thinking control 163; tolerance of uncertainty 143–5, 150, 152

acceptance beliefs 4, 8, 30, 61–86; absence of positive aspect of life 65–8; determination of 73–4; external control 161–2; flexibility 79; helpful nature of 79; logical nature of 77–9; negative aspects of life 62–5, 68–70, 71–3; negative connotations of acceptance 61–2; realistic unconditional acceptance credos 80–5; resilience 137, 138; self-control 170–1; self-discipline 117–18; tolerance of uncertainty 154; truth 75–7; working towards a goal 80; *see also* life-acceptance beliefs; other-acceptance beliefs; self-acceptance beliefs

action, taking 109–10

action tendencies: acceptance/depreciation beliefs 73; awfulising/non-awfulising beliefs 36; behavioural control 162, 167; discomfort tolerance/intolerance beliefs 53; resilience 131–2; tolerance of uncertainty 150

active preferences 11

adversity ('A') 1, 3; acceptance beliefs 61–2, 80–1, 82–3; behavioural control 163; discomfort tolerance beliefs 51–2, 54–5, 58–9; evaluation of badness 32; external control 159–60; flexible vs. rigid beliefs 14–16; non-awfulising beliefs 40, 41; resilience 119–20, 121, 123, 126, 127–8, 132–4, 136–9; 'rolling with the punches' 19–20; situational ABC framework 118–19, 127–8; thinking control 164; tolerance of uncertainty 150, 152

alcohol 98–9, 100, 123, 124

anger: healthy 40, 57, 79; internal control 163; tackling disturbance 2

anxiety: awfulising beliefs 33; discomfort intolerance beliefs 47, 48; health-related 147–8; internal control 165; performance 125; preferences 9–10; public speaking 2–3

assertiveness 160–1

avoidance 122

awfulising beliefs 7, 41; awfulising component 34; determination of 36–7; evaluation of badness component 32–3, 34; realistic non-awfulising credo 42, 43; resilience 136; self-control 170; self-discipline 117; tolerance of uncertainty 144, 152, 153, 155

badness, evaluation of 30–3, 34, 35–6, 38, 39–40
Becket, Thomas à 96
behavioural consequences: acceptance beliefs 73, 79; awfulising beliefs 36; behavioural control 163; depreciation beliefs 73; discomfort intolerance beliefs 53; discomfort tolerance beliefs 53, 57; external control 159–60; flexible vs. rigid beliefs 15, 17, 18–19; non-awfulising beliefs 36, 40; resilience 131–2; thinking control 163; tolerance of uncertainty 144, 145, 150, 152
behavioural control 162–3, 167
beliefs ('B'): behavioural control 163, 167; external control 159–60; health-related concerns 147, 148–9; resilience 128, 132, 134; situational ABC framework 118–19, 128; thinking control 162; tolerance of uncertainty 143–5, 150–1, 152; see also extreme beliefs; flexible beliefs; irrational beliefs; non-extreme beliefs; rational beliefs; rigid beliefs
bereavement 121, 122
birthdays, forgetting 65–8
'bouncing back' 121, 132, 134
bravery 122–3

change 20–2; absence of positive aspect of life 67, 68; negative aspects of life 64, 65, 69–70, 72, 73; resilience 120, 130, 132–3, 135, 138–9; self-acceptance beliefs 137
child psychology 126
cognitive behaviour therapy (CBT) 90
cognitive consequences see thinking consequences
commitment 109
complexity: flexible beliefs 22–4; resilience 138; self-control 170; uncertainty 156

concern: acceptance beliefs 79; discomfort tolerance beliefs 48, 57; flexible beliefs 10; health-related 147; non-awfulising beliefs 33, 40; tolerance of uncertainty 145, 152
consequences ('C') 119; behavioural control 163; external control 157–8; resilience 120, 129–32, 134; thinking control 164; tolerance of uncertainty 144, 144, 150, 152; see also behavioural consequences; emotional consequences; thinking consequences
control 158–72; courage 159–60; definition of 158–9; Eastern approach 166–7, 169; external vs. internal 159; losing internal 162–5; Paradoxical approach 166, 168–9; realistic rational self-control credo 169–72; serenity 160–2; Western approach 166, 168
courage 159–60
creativity 24–6
criticism from boss 62–5

denial: realistic discomfort tolerance credo 59, 60; realistic flexibility credo 27, 28; realistic non-awfulising credo 41, 43; realistic unconditional acceptance credos 81, 82, 84, 85; resilience 136, 138, 139; tolerance of uncertainty 155, 156
depreciation beliefs 7, 80–1; absence of positive aspect of life 66; determination of 73–4; life-depreciation beliefs 63–4, 66, 84–5, 138, 156, 171; negative aspects of life 63–4; other-depreciation beliefs 71, 72, 83, 137–8; resilience 137; self-control 170–1; self-depreciation beliefs 69, 78, 81–2, 84, 117–18, 137, 156, 170–1; self-discipline 117–18; tolerance of uncertainty 156

depression 15, 37, 53, 74, 78
development problems 1, 2–3
disappointment: acceptance beliefs
78, 79; discomfort tolerance
beliefs 57; non-awfulising beliefs
40
discomfort, types of 46–7
discomfort intolerance beliefs 7;
determination of 53–4; intensity
of discomfort 46; intolerance
component 48, 49; realistic
discomfort tolerance credo 59,
60; resilience 137; self-control
170; self-discipline 117; struggle
component 47–8, 49; tolerance
of uncertainty 155–6
discomfort tolerance beliefs 3, 8,
30, 44–60; determination of
53–4; flexibility 57–8; health-
related concerns 147; helpful
nature of 57; logical nature of
56; realistic discomfort
tolerance credo 58–60;
resilience 137; self-control 170;
self-discipline 117; struggle
component 44–8, 50–1, 55, 56;
tolerance of uncertainty 156;
toleration component 47–8,
49–51, 55, 56; truth 54–6;
working towards a goal 58;
'worth it' component 47–8,
51–2, 55
dissatisfaction problems 1–2
disturbance: evaluation of badness
32; realistic discomfort
tolerance credo 59, 60; realistic
flexibility credo 27, 28; realistic
non-awfulising credo 41, 43;
realistic rational self-motivation
credo 106; realistic
unconditional acceptance
credos 82, 83–4, 85; resilience
136, 138–9; self-control 169,
171, 172; self-discipline 118,
119; tackling 1–3; tolerance of
uncertainty 142, 156, 157;
unmet demands 9
drugs 98–9, 100, 124

Ellis, Albert 7, 26
emotional consequences:
behavioural control 163; external
control 159–60; flexible vs. rigid
beliefs 10, 14–15, 17, 18;
resilience 129–31; self-acceptance
beliefs 78; self-depreciation
beliefs 78; thinking control 164;
tolerance of uncertainty 144, 145,
150, 152; see also healthy negative
emotions; unhealthy negative
emotions
emotional control 164–5, 167
emotional pain 121–2, 123, 124,
132–3, 135
encounter groups 2
envy, healthy 40, 57, 79
Epictetus 134
esteem needs 104
'executive self' (ES) 108, 111–12
'experiential avoidance' 122
extreme beliefs: evaluation of
badness 33, 36; resilience 138;
self-control 171; self-discipline
118; struggle component 51;
tolerance of uncertainty 150; see
also awfulising beliefs;
depreciation beliefs; discomfort
intolerance beliefs; irrational
beliefs; rigid beliefs

fear of flying 145–6
feeling-based motivation 101–3, 105
Flach, F. 120
flexible beliefs 3, 7–29; absence of
positive aspect of life 66, 67;
behavioural consequences 15, 17,
18–19; cognitive consequences
16, 17, 19; determination of 14;
emotional consequences 14–15,
17, 18; external control 159–60;
health-related concerns 147;
helpful nature of 18–19;
importance of flexibility 19–26;
logical nature of 18; motivation
99–100, 101–2, 103; negative
aspects of life 63, 65, 68, 70, 71,
72; non-rigid component 10,
11–14, 18; preferential

component 8–11, 12, 13–14, 18; realistic flexibility credo 27–9; resilience 128, 138; self-control 169, 171; self-discipline 116, 118; 'subsequent thinking' 132; tolerance of uncertainty 144, 150, 152–3, 155, 156; truth 17; working towards flexibility as a goal 26–7
flying, fear of 143–4
Freud, Sigmund 95

goals: acceptance beliefs 80; achievement 110; discomfort tolerance beliefs 58; flexibility 26–7; introjected 90–1; long-term 92–3, 107–8, 110–12, 116, 117, 124–5; non-awfulising beliefs 41; outcome and process 91; positive and negative 90; resilience 135; self-discipline 107, 108–9; short-term 92–3, 97–9, 107, 111, 116, 125; tolerance of uncertainty 150, 152–3
guilt 23–4

happiness 55
health-related concerns 147–9
healthy negative emotions (HNEs): acceptance beliefs 73, 79; discomfort tolerance beliefs 53, 57, 59; flexible beliefs 14–15, 17, 18, 27; non-awfulising beliefs 36, 40, 42; resilience 136; self-control 167; tolerance of uncertainty 150, 152, 155
hierarchy of needs 3, 103–4

improvement 108–10
inferences 16
introjection 90, 91
intrusive thoughts 164–5
irrational beliefs 7; health-related concerns 149; 'subsequent thinking' 132; tolerance of uncertainty 150–1, 153–4; Western approach to internal control 168; see also awfulising beliefs; depreciation beliefs;

discomfort intolerance beliefs; rigid beliefs

jealousy, healthy 40, 57, 79

Laing, R.D. 120
life-acceptance beliefs: absence of positive aspect of life 65–8; negative aspects of life 62–5; realistic unconditional life-acceptance credo 83–5; resilience 138; self-control 171; tolerance of uncertainty 156
life-depreciation beliefs: absence of positive aspect of life 66; negative aspects of life 63–4; realistic unconditional life-acceptance credo 84–5; resilience 138; self-control 171; tolerance of uncertainty 156
'long-term self' (LTS) 108, 110–11, 112–13

Maslow, Abraham 3, 26, 103–4
meditation 163–4
motivation 89–106; conscious and unconscious 95; definition of healthy 104–5; discomfort tolerance beliefs 51–2; doing things for others 90–1, 94–5; feelings 101–3; goals 90–2; hierarchy of needs 103–4; mixed 94; realistic rational self-motivation credo 105–6; reasons 89–101, 102–3, 104–5; rigid vs. flexible 99–100; time-frames 92–3; values and principles 95–9, 100, 104–5

needs, hierarchy of 3, 103–4
negative preferences 8–9, 31, 45
non-awfulising beliefs 3, 8, 30–43; anti-awfulising component 33, 34–6, 38, 39; determination of 36–7; evaluation of badness component 30–3, 35, 38, 39–40; flexibility 40; health-related concerns 147; helpful nature of 40; logical nature of 39–40;

realistic non-awfulising credo
41–3; resilience 136–7; self-
control 170; self-discipline 117;
tolerance of uncertainty 144,
152–3, 155; truth 38–9; working
towards a goal 41
non-extreme beliefs: evaluation of
badness 32–3, 35–6, 39–40;
external control 159–60; realistic
discomfort tolerance credo 59;
realistic non-awfulising credo 42;
realistic unconditional acceptance
credos 81, 82, 83, 84; resilience
128, 138; self-control 171; self-
discipline 118; struggle
component 50, 51, 56; tolerance
of uncertainty 150, 152–3, 156;
see also acceptance beliefs;
discomfort tolerance beliefs;
flexible beliefs; non-awfulising
beliefs; rational beliefs
novelty 22

other-acceptance beliefs 70–3, 75–6,
82–3, 138
other-depreciation beliefs 71, 72, 83,
137–8
outcome goals 91
overt behaviour 131–2, 162, 167

part-whole error 78
passive preferences 11
perfectionism 121
positive preferences 8–9, 31, 45
preferences 8–11; active vs. passive
11; discomfort tolerance beliefs
45; evaluation of badness 31, 32;
full and part 13–14
principles 95–9, 100, 104–5
process activities 91–2
psychotic breakdown 120

rational beliefs: behavioural control
163, 167; emotional control 165;
external control 160, 161–2;
health-related concerns 147, 148,
149; 'subsequent thinking' 132;
tolerance of uncertainty 143,
150–1, 153–4; Western approach

to internal control 168; see also
acceptance beliefs; discomfort
tolerance beliefs; flexible beliefs;
non-awfulising beliefs; non-
extreme beliefs
Rational Emotive Behaviour
Therapy (REBT) 1, 7, 26;
acceptance 64, 67; evaluation of
badness 32; preferences 9, 10;
situational ABC framework
118–19, 127–32
rationalisation 116, 117, 119
realistic discomfort tolerance credo
58–60
realistic flexibility credo 27–9
realistic non-awfulising credo 41–3
realistic rational resilience credo
135–9
realistic rational self-control credo
169–72
realistic rational self-motivation
credo 105–6
realistic rational tolerance of
uncertainty credo 154–7
realistic self-discipline credo 115–19
realistic unconditional acceptance
credos 80–5
reasons 89–101, 102–3; definition of
healthy motivation 104–5; goals
and 90–2; passive vs. active 101;
real vs. expressed 93–5; values
and principles 95–9
REBT see Rational Emotive
Behaviour Therapy
remorse: acceptance beliefs 79;
discomfort tolerance beliefs 57;
non-awfulising beliefs 40
resilience 118–39; behaviour ratio
126; behavioural consequences
131–2; common view of 118–26;
definition of 132–5; emotional
consequences 129–31; emotional
pain 121–2, 123, 124, 132–3, 135;
learning 134; realistic rational
resilience credo 135–9; restraint
123–5; situational ABC
framework 127–32; struggle
122–3, 125, 132–3, 135; thinking
consequences 132

rigid beliefs 7; as barrier to creativity 24–5; behavioural consequences 15, 17; cognitive consequences 16, 17; determination of 14; emotional consequences 14–15, 17; motivation 99–100, 102, 103, 105; preferential component 9–10, 12, 13; realistic flexibility credo 27–8; resilience 138; resistance to change 20–2; response to adversity 20; rigid component 11–12; self-control 169, 171; self-discipline 116, 118; simplicity 22–3; 'subsequent thinking' 132; tolerance of uncertainty 143–5, 150, 152, 155
risk 9, 31, 45

sadness 37, 54, 74; acceptance beliefs 79; discomfort tolerance beliefs 57; flexible beliefs 15; non-awfulising beliefs 40
self-acceptance beliefs 68–70, 74; component analysis 76–7, 78; logical nature of 77–9; realistic unconditional self-acceptance credo 80–2; resilience 137, 138; self-control 170–1; self-discipline 117–18; truth 75–7; uncertainty 156
self-actualisation 3, 26, 104, 126
self-control 156–70; courage 157–8; definition of control 156–7; Eastern approach 164–5, 167; external vs. internal control 157; losing internal control 160–3; Paradoxical approach 164, 166–7; realistic rational self-control credo 167–70; serenity 158–60; Western approach 164, 166
self-deceit 116
self-depreciation beliefs 69, 78, 82, 84; resilience 137; self-control 170–1; self-discipline 117–18; uncertainty 156
self-discipline 47, 107–17; definition of 107–8; 'executive self' 108,

111–12; goals 126; improvement 108–10; 'long-term self' 108, 110–11, 112–13; obstacles 108; realistic self-discipline credo 115–19; 'short-term self' 108, 111
self-esteem 126
self-motivation 89–106; conscious and unconscious 95; definition of healthy motivation 104–5; doing things for others 90–1, 94–5; feelings 101–3; goals 90–2; mixed motives 94; realistic rational self-motivation credo 105–6; rigid vs. flexible 99–100; time-frames 92–3; values and principles 95–9
self-worth 52
serenity 160–2
'short-term self' (STS) 108, 111
situational ABC framework 118–19, 127–32; behavioural control 163; external control 159–60; thinking control 164; tolerance of uncertainty 143–5, 150, 152
situational resilience 119
sorrow: acceptance beliefs 79; discomfort tolerance beliefs 57; non-awfulising beliefs 40
'subsequent thinking' 132

thinking (cognitive) consequences: acceptance beliefs 73, 79; awfulising beliefs 37; behavioural control 161; depreciation beliefs 74; discomfort intolerance beliefs 53; discomfort tolerance beliefs 53, 57; flexible vs. rigid beliefs 16, 17, 19; non-awfulising beliefs 36, 40; resilience 132; thinking control 164; tolerance of uncertainty 144, 145, 150, 152
thinking control 163–4, 166–7
threats 142, 154; external control 159–60; health-related concerns 147–9; worry 141–3; see also adversity
trait resilience 119
truth: acceptance beliefs 75–7; discomfort tolerance beliefs 54–6;

flexible beliefs 17; non-awfulising beliefs 38–9

uncertainty, tolerance of 142–57; fear of flying 145–6; health-related concerns 147–9; healthy goals 150, 152–3; identification of problem 149–50, 152; rational/irrational beliefs 150–1, 153–4; realistic rational tolerance of uncertainty credo 154–7; worry 143–5
unconditional life-acceptance (ULA): absence of positive aspect of life 65–8; negative aspect of life 62–5; realistic unconditional life-acceptance credo 83–5; truth 75–6
unconditional other-acceptance (UOA) 70–3; realistic

unconditional other-acceptance credo 82–3; truth 75–6
unconditional self-acceptance (USA) 68–70; component analysis 76–7, 78; logical nature of 77–9; realistic unconditional self-acceptance credo 80–2; truth 75–7
the unconscious 95
unhealthy negative emotions (UNEs): awfulising beliefs 36; depreciation beliefs 73; discomfort intolerance beliefs 53; realistic self-discipline credo 116; rigid beliefs 14–15, 17; tolerance of uncertainty 150

values 95–9, 100, 104–5

worry 143–5